# AN INTERNATIONAL ECONOMIC SYSTEM

BY

## J. J. POLAK

THE UNIVERSITY OF CHICAGO PRESS
CHICAGO · ILLINOIS

THE UNIVERSITY OF CHICAGO PRESS, CHICAGO 37
George Allen & Unwin, Ltd., London W.C.1, England

PRINTED IN GREAT BRITAIN
BY WILLIAM BRENDON AND SON, LTD.
THE MAYFLOWER PRESS (LATE OF PLYMOUTH)
WATFORD, HERTS.

# PREFACE

THE idea underlying this study is a very simple one. It aims at showing how certain elementary relationships, the significance of which in national economies is already well-known, can be transferred to the field of international trade. The experience of the 'thirties taught us the importance of effective demand as a factor determining the sales of different industries in the home market; this study stresses the effects of the same factor, effective demand, upon sales by different countries in world markets. In the last fifteen years investment expenditure has come to be regarded, probably exaggeratedly so, as the autonomous factor which determines the rest of aggregate demand and as the lever by which the entire economy can be lifted. In economies heavily dependent on foreign trade, it is clear that exports are an autonomous factor influencing the level of activity in much the same manner as investment, and of at least the same, and probably of much greater importance. Moreover, while exports are to a large extent an autonomous variable when looked at from the point of view of the exporting country, they are not autonomous when considered in the framework of a study which encompasses the entire world. In this wider framework, exports are seen as determined mainly by factors in the importing countries, in particular by the fluctuations in income in these countries. Thus a link is established between the chains of causation of various national economies, and the outline of an international economic system emerges.

So much for the theoretical origins of the study. Its purpose, however, is not merely to construct a plausible theoretical model of the world economy; it is also to adduce evidence of the relation of the model to reality. For this reason an attempt has been made to give statistical content to the system on the basis of empirical data relating to the inter-war period. For some twenty-five countries statistical relationships have been fitted among the relevant variables such as exports, national income, imports, relative prices of foreign and domestic goods, etc.

Chapter I provides a bird's eye view of the system. Chapters II, III and IV develop in further detail the various elements of the system with special attention to the underlying more complicated relationships that are condensed in the simplified structure of the statistical model. Some readers may prefer to skip these chapters (which are in places a little more difficult than the rest of the book), at least in part, proceeding at once from Chapter I to Chapter V, where the condensed relationships are fitted together, and from there to the statistical section.

The author is, and was when preparing this study in the years 1947 to 1949, an official of the International Monetary Fund, but the opinions expressed are, of course, in no sense official. During the greater part of the work, the author had the good fortune of being assisted by Mr. Tse Chun Chang, then an economist in the Research Department of the Fund, who supervised most of the work on individual countries and made valuable contributions to the theoretical sections. The author also wants to express his thanks to Mr. Sidney S. Alexander, of the Fund, for his helpful criticism.

J. J. POLAK

Washington, D.C.
*December 1951*

# CONTENTS

# CONTENTS

# CONTENTS

# CHAPTER I

# AN OUTLINE OF THE SYSTEM

THE national economies of the various countries mesh into an international economic system through the media of international trade, international capital movements and other international transactions. Through these same channels economic fluctuations occurring within each of the economic systems of the various countries are transmitted from one country to another. By reference to the economic relationships which determine the fluctuations in international trade and other international magnitudes, the economic models which describe the economies of individual countries may be linked together into one economic system describing the economic fluctuations in the world as a whole.

The objective of this study is to approach—first theoretically and then statistically—this "international economic system". The need for a working knowledge of this international economic system is paramount. National governments and international agencies apply and recommend a multitude of international economic policies—policies affecting tariffs, exchange rates, the volume of international trade, international capital movements, etc. The effects of these policies make themselves felt through the world economy. They pass from country to country in a manner which can be described only by a number of international economic relationships. Hence an intelligent judgment of past policies and a wise framing of future policies require knowledge, as accurate as we can obtain, of these international economic relationships.

For a few countries dynamic economic models exist which describe the mechanism of fluctuation of the domestic economies of these countries. One might conceivably arrive at an international economic model by pushing farther along this road, constructing for one country after another a similar dynamic economic model. Through the foreign trade relationships in each such model these various country models could then ultimately be tied together into an international model. But anyone who has had any experience in the construction of a model of this nature for the economy of one country will know that this course of action would be both long and unrewarding. It would take years to construct even tolerably adequate models for, say, a dozen individual countries; and unless these models had been specifically constructed to reflect the countries' foreign relationships they might not be sufficiently reliable to be used for international linking, even though they gave a reasonably good description of the economy of the country concerned. For the great majority of countries, moreover, any attempt to construct a complete model would falter on the lack of statistics. It would seem more profitable therefore at the present stage of statistical knowledge to construct directly an international economic model. In doing so we can benefit from the fortuitous fact that the indicators of the most important international relationships, namely trade statistics, have been recorded with much greater accuracy and detail for decades and sometimes centuries, than statistics on almost any other economic phenomenon of similar importance.

Logically an international economic model is not different from a national model. It is free from the awkwardness of national models which almost always stop at a country's boundaries where revenue from exports comes in as an unexplained foreign factor and payments for imports go out as a loose end, caused by the national economy under consideration but going no-where in particular. If we aim directly at an international economic model we may have to forgo consideration of many interesting details in the national economies, but we gain much: a picture, however rough, of the inter-national operation of the world as a whole as an economic system. With respect to individual countries, too, we find that for the great majority the relations with the out-side world are far more important as prime movers of the fluctuations in the national economy than those prime movers of national origin to which attention has been primarily focused in recent literature: domestic invest-ment and government finance.

An attempt to cover the whole world, or at least a very large proportion of it, in one economic model entails inevitably a heavy degree of simplification. In its sim-plest terms the approach which will be used may be described by reference to the diagram on page 16. This diagram is still somewhat simpler than the treatment in the text in the succeeding chapters, in particular by the omission of any reference to changes in relative prices and their effects. The diagram may be read starting in any one point. If we commence at the top of the diagram moving along the arrows, we find the four following basic relationships:

(1) Fluctuations in the level of a country's exports bring about fluctuations in its domestic activity and hence in its national income. In part this relationship is instantaneous, an increase in ex-ports constituting an increase in national income and in part it works with a certain lag *via* the multiplier.

(2) Fluctuations in national income influence the level of imports either at the same time or with a certain time lag.

THE INTERNATIONAL ECONOMIC SYSTEM

(3) By definition the total of the imports of all countries equals the total volume of world trade.

(4) The total volume of world trade as given in any
one year is distributed over the $n$ countries which
constitute the world, and the volume of exports
of each country is assumed to be determined by
the level of world trade.

This closes the circle.[1] If this were all, an equilibrium
situation would (under certain conditions) establish
itself with given values for the level of trade and the
national income of all countries; there would be no fluctuations. Actually fluctuations do occur because income
is determined not only by exports but also by certain
"autonomous factors"; similarly imports are determined
not only by income but also by some autonomous factors.
These factors which may be operative in each of the $n$
countries, are symbolically indicated in the diagram.
Among the autonomous factors one may consider for
instance autonomous investment and autonomous fluctuations in government finance as factors affecting national
income, and crop fluctuations or measures of commercial
policy as factors affecting imports directly.

The autonomous factors are the prime movers of the
whole system. If a given new level for all autonomous
factors in all countries were to persist for a sufficiently
long time, an equilibrium level of trade and income
would again establish itself in each country corresponding to that particular level of all the autonomous factors.
Changes in the level of the various autonomous factors

[1] Another exposition in which the third and fourth relationships are combined
may be preferred. One might say that fluctuations in the national income of any
one country determine the imports of that country from any other country.
Accordingly one would have to draw the arrows directly from the import of any
one country to the exports of all other countries. The interposition of the total of
world trade between imports and exports reduces, however, greatly the number of
arrows in the diagram and, more importantly, it reduces in the same manner the
number of relationships which have to be studied. It will be seen readily that this
number is reduced from $n(n-1)$ to $2n$ if the method of exposition selected in the
diagram is followed.

will determine changes in trade and national income; and if the sum total of the autonomous factors (appropriately weighted) fluctuates, trade and income in all countries will fluctuate in unison with this total.

In describing and analysing the peculiarities of a system two emphases are possible. One may either concentrate on a description of the prime movers and consider the mechanism as a sort of multiplier which simply enlarges the fluctuations basically due to the prime movers. Or alternatively one may concentrate on the system of transmission and pay rather less attention to the autonomous factors, then rather called "shocks", that are transmitted by the system. In the present study the latter emphasis will dominate. In taking this approach we concentrate on what is relatively stable and lasting as against a description of one-time historical occurrences. As mentioned above, knowledge of the system, rather than of the fluctuations which it happened to transmit in the past, is what we require in connection with questions of economic policy in the future.

Granted then the abstraction, in our description, from autonomous factors, it will be necessary to point out that even in the portrayal of the systematic elements we cannot attempt or hope to be complete. We cannot grasp the full system with its infinite complications of responses of millions of economic subjects. Inevitably, we must work with a simplified model, and select one particular model out of the great number of possible models. It is believed that the particular model around which this study is organized contains the main characteristic features of reality. The high correlation coefficients obtained provide some assurance of its realism. Nevertheless there may be other systematic elements which, at times, may have been quite important, which have not been incorporated in our model.

A further important limitation presents itself immediately. In order to measure the characteristics of any economic system time series over a relatively long period are required. In the present study these time series have been derived from the interwar period, which is itself a relatively short span of time to constitute the basis for the measurement of coefficients in economic relationships; not infrequently even this short period had to be broken into two parts, roughly the '20's and the '30's. The results found in this study refer therefore to a time before World War II and they cannot without reconsideration be applied to the present world. They are nonetheless believed to be valuable because they throw a somewhat new light on the international economic system as it existed in the '20's and the '30's (and on the differences between these two decades); and they constitute a framework which, with relatively simple adaptation, could be made suitable to describe the postwar situation as soon as the pattern of economic behaviour of individual countries has settled down to a state of relative stability.

The organization of the study follows closely the outline of the system which was indicated in the diagram, starting at its top. First we study the relation between foreign factors and national income (Chapter II); then the relation between imports and national income (Chapter III). Thereafter we explain the volume of exports of individual countries as a function of world trade (Chapter IV) and then tie together the findings of the individual chapters into an international economic system in Chapter V. In the second, statistical, part, we measure the relationships established in the first part and draw certain conclusions with respect to the system as a whole.

# CHAPTER II

# THE RELATION BETWEEN FOREIGN FACTORS AND NATIONAL INCOME

## 1. THE FOREIGN TRADE MULTIPLIER

THE impact of foreign factors upon the national income of a country has frequently been studied by use of the concept of the "foreign trade multiplier".[1] This concept may be used here as a convenient starting-point. In its simplest form, the theory of the foreign trade multiplier may be presented in a few basic equations.

The first equation defines income produced ($Y$) as the sum of the value of output of final goods for domestic consumption ($C$), home investment ($V$) and exports ($X$), minus the value of imports ($M$) contained in the three former:

$$Y = C + V + X - M \qquad (21 \cdot 1)$$

The second and third equations state that both consumption and imports are a linear function of income, but not a proportional function, as both contain constant terms ($C_o$ and $M_o$):

$$C = \gamma^* Y + C_o \qquad (21 \cdot 2)$$
$$M = \mu^* Y + M_o \qquad (21 \cdot 3)$$

In these two equations, $\gamma^*$ stands for the marginal propensity to consume and $\mu^*$ for the marginal propensity to import.[2] Both equations might have a certain lag

---

[1] *See* J. J. Polak, "The Foreign Trade Multiplier", *American Economic Review*, Vol. XXXVII, December 1947, page 889, and earlier sources mentioned there.

[2] The coefficients $\gamma^*$ and $\mu^*$ carry an asterisk to save the coefficients $\gamma$ and $\mu$ for later use.

but for reasons set out below (Section 5 below) no account is being taken of such possible lags in the presentation of these and the following equations.

Disregarding, for the time being, $V$, and substituting $(21 \cdot 2)$ and $(21 \cdot 3)$ into $(21 \cdot 1)$, one derives an equation of $\varUpsilon$ as a function of $X$ and a constant term:

$$\varUpsilon = \frac{X}{1 - \gamma^* + \mu^*} - \frac{C_o - M_o}{1 - \gamma^* + \mu^*} \qquad (21 \cdot 4)$$

The fraction $\dfrac{1}{1 - \gamma^* + \mu^*}$ is the "foreign trade multiplier", indicating the relation between an increase (or decrease) in the rate of national income $\varUpsilon$ and an increase (or decrease) in the rate of exports $X$ by which it is caused.

The variables $\varUpsilon$, $C$, etc., might be taken as money values or as real values (money values at constant prices). For both the consumption and the import equation it would seem more reasonable to assume that they are relatively constant in real terms, rather than in money terms. For the consumption equation this implies that one assumes the absence of a "money illusion". For the import equation the complimentarity of many imported goods (in particular raw materials) to the volume of output of consumption and export goods provides a reason for assuming a constant marginal propensity to import in real, rather than in money, terms.[1] On the basis of the

---

[1] Lord Keynes' views on the subject may be referred to, as given in a letter to Mr. Colin Clark:

"I can see no possible advantage in your calculation in terms of money undeflated by wages or prices. There is surely a greater presumption of stability of marginal propensity to consume or to import in terms of wage units or composite commodity units than in terms of money. In fact the Australian figures do not work out at all well on the assumption of a stable marginal propensity to consume in terms of money; though I cannot say whether the correspondence would look better if you were to deflate money by reference to wage units."

(Colin Clark and J. C. Crawford, *The National Income of Australia*, Sydney, 1938, page 92, *n.* 1.)

assumptions made, we may write as the "real" equivalents of (21·2) and (21·3):

$$c = \gamma y + c_o \qquad (21·5)$$
$$m = \mu y + m_o \qquad (21·6)$$

where the lower-case symbols ($c$, $m$ and $y$) stand for the
real equivalents of the values indicated by capitals (the
volume of consumption, the volume of imports, and real
national income), and $\gamma$ and $\mu$ (without asterisks) refer
explicitly to "real" propensities. The distinction between
money and real magnitudes introduces, at the same time,
the concept of price indices and the possibility of a diver-
gent movement of different prices. Allowance has to be
made, therefore, for the effect of changes in the terms of
trade on national income. The consequent adjustment
required to equation (21·4) follows directly from our
definition of real income, as given in the following
paragraph.

## 2. THE EFFECT OF CHANGES IN IMPORT AND EXPORT PRICES ON REAL INCOME

We define real national income ($y$) as the purchasing
power of money national income ($Y$) over consumption
goods.

We can then prove[1] that with a high degree of
approximation the following holds as long as $X$ approxi-
mates $M$:

$$y = x \frac{p_x}{p_m} + c - m \qquad (22·1)$$

where $p_x$ is the export price index and $p_m$ the import price
index.

We find, in other words, that the fluctuations in real

[1] *See* Annex I.

national income consist of a foreign part and a domestic part. The foreign part is the volume of exports $(x)$ times the terms of trade $\left(\dfrac{p_x}{p_m}\right)$ or the value of exports divided by the import price index $\left(\dfrac{X}{p_m}\right)$; and the domestic part $(c - m)$ is the total volume of consumption minus the volume of imports which enters into it, or the real value added in the domestic production of consumption goods.

A numerical example will readily make clear why the value of exports and the import price index enter in this particular combination. Assume a country has a national income of 1,000 and exports and imports of 200 each. Now an increase of its exports by 20 units (*i.e.* by 10 per cent) increases its money national income, and, all other things being equal, its real national income also, by the same 20 units, or 2 per cent. A fall of the import price index by 10 per cent has exactly the same effect on real national income: since imports are 20 per cent of national income, a 10 per cent price fall in imports will be reflected in a 2 per cent price fall of the general price level, *i.e.* a 2 per cent rise in real income.

For simplicity the foreign factors will be indicated by the symbol $f$:

$$f = \frac{X}{p_m} = x\frac{p_x}{p_m} \qquad (22 \cdot 2)$$

For some countries it is necessary to use an alternative series for $f$, derived in a slightly different fashion (see Annex I). This alternative series is indicated as $f'$.

It is necessary to bear in mind at this stage that the effect of foreign factors on real income as indicated by $(22 \cdot 1)$ is both *partial* and *primary* only. It is partial because it does not reflect the effect on income resulting from a change in the volume of imports in response to a change in the relative cost of imports. Such changes in income will be taken into consideration when we assume a more complicated import formula than (21·6); our present formula assumes zero elasticity of substitution between imports and domestic production. It is primary because the multiplier effects have not yet been taken into consideration. We proceed to do this now. Using (21·5), (21·6), (22·1), and (22·2) we obtain:

$$y = f + c_o - m_o + y(\gamma - \mu)$$

or:

$$y = \frac{f}{1 - \gamma + \mu} + \frac{c_o - m_o}{1 - \gamma + \mu} \qquad (22 \cdot 3)$$

The last term is a constant and may be replaced by $y_o$; we can then write:

$$y = \frac{f}{1 - \gamma + \mu} + y_o \qquad (22 \cdot 4)$$

where $\dfrac{1}{1 - \gamma + \mu}$ is again the foreign trade multiplier.

## 3. IMPORTS FOR CONSUMPTION AND IMPORTS FOR INVESTMENT

We may now expand our analysis to eliminate some of the simplifying assumptions made earlier. In the first place we introduce domestic investment $(V)$. To do so we split imports into imports for the production of domestic consumption goods $(M_c)$ and imports for the production of investment goods $(M_v)$.

$$M = M_c + M_v \qquad (23 \cdot 1)$$

Then $(C - M_c)$ is the value added domestically in the production of consumption goods and $(V - M_v)$ is the value added domestically in the production of investment goods, $(c - m_c)$ the volume of domestic output of consumption goods and $(v - m_v)$ the volume of domestic output of investment goods.

If we may now make two assumptions, viz.:

(a) that
$$\frac{M_v}{V} = \frac{M_c}{C}$$

and

(b) that the fluctuations in the price level relating to the domestic value added of consumer goods and investments goods is the same—that is, in practice, that the wage levels in consumption goods industries and producer goods industries move parallel, we may write, with the same approximation as that used in arriving at (22·1):

$$y = f + c + v - m \qquad (23·2)$$

It may readily be pointed out that the assumptions made (equal import proportion and parallel wage movement for consumer and producer goods) are not likely to be strictly true for any one country and may be shown to be quite inaccurate for many a country. This objection is, however, not as serious as it might seem at first glance. Usually, $C$ is much larger than $V$ and any inaccuracies in the assumptions are proportionately very much reduced in the way in which they appear in any weighted average.

## 4. INDUCED INVESTMENT

In order to reduce (23·2) to an equation simply between the variables $y$ and $f$ it will be necessary to "explain" not only $c$ and $m$ but also $v$. The most convenient way of achieving this is to postulate an equation

$$v = \varphi y + v_o \qquad (24·1)$$

where $\varphi$ would be the "marginal propensity to invest", and the multiplier would be $\dfrac{1}{1 - \varphi - \gamma + \mu}$ :

$$y = \frac{f}{1 - \varphi - \gamma + \mu} + \frac{v_o + c_o - m_o}{1 - \varphi - \gamma + \mu} \qquad (24\cdot2)$$

As a rough approximation, an equation like $(24\cdot1)$ may serve. Clearly the volume of investment, like the volume of consumption, fluctuates with business conditions in general, and so does real national income. Yet it would seem that, in many cases, a more refined explanation of investment would be required, bringing in profits, rates of profit, rates of interest, prices of producer goods and possibly, according to the "acceleration principle", the rate of increase of the production of consumption goods. In such a situation, an approximate equation like $(24\cdot1)$ and the multiplier based on it might not appear acceptable.

The objection raised, can, however, be met, without complicating the system of equations we have to work with statistically, even though the full system describing the entire economy contains a great number of variables. Only one additional condition is necessary; *viz.* that all relationships between these variables can adequately be represented by *linear* relations. In general the statistical results achieved with linear relations have been so satisfactory in economics that it would not seem unreasonable to operate on the assumption that this condition is, in general, fulfilled. If this is so, it can readily be seen that any complicated set of relationships involving $v, y$ and a number of other relevant economic variables can be reduced to one linear equation between $v$ and $y$. Equation $(24\cdot1)$ would then represent a derived rather than a direct equation. Although $\varphi$ can now no longer be called the "marginal propensity to invest", it does represent the marginal effect on investment of a change in income.

The multiplier equation (24·2) then also stands unchanged.

Since the combination of coefficients $(1 - \varphi - \gamma + \mu)$ will have to be used much in the following, it is convenient to write it in a somewhat shorter form, while still keeping $\mu$ explicit. We write, therefore,

$$1 - \varphi - \gamma = \delta \qquad (24·3)$$

and the multiplier as:

$$\frac{1}{\delta + \mu} \qquad (24·4)$$

If one likes, one may interpret $\delta$ as the "marginal propensity not to spend".

## 5. THE TREATMENT OF LAGS

It will be noted that time lags have been omitted throughout, although clearly not all of the equations can describe instantaneous adjustments. The basis for this omission is not that all the lags involved may be taken as negligible, but rather that for our purpose—the presentation of a system which indicates the impact of foreign factors on the economy of a country and the resulting reactions on the rest of the world—the time lags are of secondary importance. The ultimate value of the multiplier, which indicates the equilibrium value of a country's national income which will be approximated for a given value of the foreign factors, is independent of the existence or the magnitude of lags.[1] This can be shown as follows.

Assume we have a general system of linear difference equations describing the economy of a country which,

[1] The lags do influence the speed and the manner (cyclically or asymptotically) in which the equilibrium value will be approached.

after elimination of all variables except $y$, gives a final equation:

$$y_t + \alpha_1 y_{t-1} + \alpha_2 y_{t-2} + \ldots\ldots\ldots \ddot{\alpha}_n y_{t-n} = A_t \qquad (25 \cdot 1)$$

where $A$ is an exogenous variable (*e.g.* in our case $A_t$ is a function of $f_t, f_{t-1} \ldots.$).

Then, if the coefficients of $(25 \cdot 1)$ are such that there exists an equilibrium value of $y$ for any value of $A$, this equilibrium value $(y_E)$ will be:

$$y_E = \frac{A}{1 + \alpha_1 + \alpha_2 \ldots. \alpha_n} \qquad (25 \cdot 2)$$

and the "multiplier" of the system with respect to $y$ will

be $\dfrac{1}{1 + \alpha_1 + \alpha_2 \ldots \alpha_n}$. It follows that, in order to find the multiplier, one may disregard the timing of the individual terms $y_t, y_{t-1} \ldots.$ and that it would have been sufficient for this purpose to have $(25 \cdot 1)$ in the compressed form:

$$(1 + \alpha_1 + \alpha_2 \ldots. + \alpha_n)y = A \qquad (25 \cdot 3)$$

But instead of operating on a system of difference equations and then compressing the final equation, one may as well present each individual equation in its compressed form, *i.e.* as an instantaneous equation. This does not affect the ultimate multiplier of the system, if there is any, *i.e.* if the system has an equilibrium value.[1]

Whether the coefficients are such that the system does, in fact, approach an equilibrium value can easily

---

[1] The statement refers to the presentation of an equation of which the coefficients are assumed to be known. It is not suggested that it would be indifferent whether lags are taken into account or not in the statistical measurement of the coefficients.

be observed from the variations of $y_t$ and $A_t$ over time. If there is a good correlation between the two series, then obviously $y$ does not react to changes in $A$ in an explosive fashion, and the coefficient found by correlating the two variables may be interpreted as the multiplier. If, on the other hand, no good correlation between the two can be found, no significant coefficient is found and there is no question as to the interpretation of any coefficient. In other words, whenever an apparent multiplier is found, it may be interpreted as *the* multiplier.[1] This conclusion is independent of the fact whether the roots corresponding to $(25 \cdot 1)$ are real or conjugate complex; it is sufficient that the movements which $(25 \cdot 1)$ describes are damped, whether they are unilateral or cyclical.

An interesting conclusion from the permissibility of "condensation" is that, for purposes of the multiplier of the system, the existence of any difference terms does not influence the multiplier as long as they do not make the system explosive. In economic terms this means that any speculative terms, indicating a reaction, *e.g.* of prices to the rate of price increase, or any acceleration terms explaining investment in terms of the rate of increase of production or sales, are without effect on the ultimate equilibrium value and do not enter into the multiplier.

## 6. WHY LAGS MAY NOT APPEAR IN THE MULTIPLIER RELATIONSHIP

Another theoretical point needs to be made, namely that it should not be expected that, because some of the relations within the country are lagged, the relation between $y$ and $f$ should necessarily be lagged. Two simplified examples may show why this need not be the case.

[1] Again, as in the previous footnote, this is a logical, not a statistical statement. Statistical data will necessarily refer to a finite period in which the equilibrium value is not fully reached, and will, therefore, always yield somewhat "truncated" multipliers.

In both examples we assume lagged consumption and import equations

$$c_t = \gamma y_{t-1} \tag{26.1}$$
$$m_t = \mu y_{t-1} \tag{26.2}$$

In the first example we assume investment to be determined by the acceleration principle. This may be written in the somewhat special form

$$v_t = \varphi(y_t - y_{t-1}) \tag{26.3}$$

with the rate of increase in the total volume of production as the determining variable.

Inserting (26.1), (26.2) and (26.3) into a definition of national income,

$$y_t = v_t + c_t + x_t - m_t \tag{26.4}$$

we find

$$y_t = \varphi(y_t - y_{t-1}) + \gamma y_{t-1} + x_t - \mu y_{t-1} \tag{26.5}$$

or:

$$(1 - \varphi)y_t + (\varphi + \mu - \gamma)y_{t-1} = x_t \tag{26.6}$$

It will be seen that if the coefficients $\varphi$, $\mu$ and $\gamma$ happen to be such that

$$\varphi + \mu - \gamma = 0, \tag{26.7}$$

then

$$(1 - \varphi)y_t = x_t \tag{26.8}$$

and $y_t$ will *not* be lagged behind $x_t$. More general, $y$ lags behind $x_t$ only if $(\varphi + \mu - \gamma) > 0$.

In the second example we assume investment to depend on current national income and prices:

$$v_t = \varphi_1 y_t - \varphi_2 p_t \quad \varphi_1, \varphi_2 > 0 \qquad (26 \cdot 9)$$

where prices have a negative influence. We further assume that prices depend on past national income, price adjustment being delayed by certain institutional rigidities:

$$p_t = \pi y_{t-1} \qquad (26 \cdot 10)$$

Substituting (26·10) into (26·9) and then substituting $v_t$ into (26·4) we find:

$$y_t (1 - \varphi_1) + y_{t-1} (\varphi_2 \pi + \mu - \gamma) = x_t \qquad (26.11)$$

Here again, no lag may appear between $y_t$ and $x_t$, provided this time that

$$\varphi_2 \pi + \mu - \gamma = 0 \qquad (26 \cdot 12)$$

Whether (26·7) and (26·12) are reasonable relations between coefficients is a question to be decided on the basis of much further analysis than can be given here. It would seem sufficient to have established at this stage that the mere fact of the existence of significant lags in some of the internal equations does not necessarily lead to the existence of a lag between $y_t$ and $f_t$ (and would not even contradict a lead). In fact little evidence is found of such a lag in our statistics.

## 7. THE TREATMENT OF AUTONOMOUS INVESTMENT

For a large number of countries, an endogenous explanation of $v$, as given in Section 4 above, would appear satisfactory, and hence the multiplier equation (24·2) with $f$ as the only exogenous variable should also be satisfactory (provided the system is damped). But in some countries a simple endogenous explanation of investment does not hold. Let us write, for such cases:

$$v = \varphi y + v_o + v_A \qquad (27·1)$$

where $v_A$ stands for autonomous investment. Accordingly (24·2) becomes [using also (22·2)]:

$$y = \left(\frac{X}{p_m} + v_A\right)\frac{1}{\delta + \mu} + y_o \qquad (27·2)$$

## 8. CAPITAL IMPORTS AND AUTONOMOUS INVESTMENT

Autonomous investment, *i.e.* investment not due to domestic factors, is particularly important in countries with little domestic saving and no organized capital market. In such countries domestic investment cannot take place on any large scale without borrowing from abroad, and is determined by the willingness of foreigners to lend. This willingness may, in certain circumstances, depend in part on economic conditions in the borrowing country and is then, to that extent, to be considered as endogenous. But conditions in the lending country always play some, and often a determining, role in the amount of foreign loans a country will receive. It seems desirable, therefore, to consider foreign loans received, and accordingly the investment conditioned by it, at least provisionally as an exogenous variable.

There is no direct connection between the amount of foreign investment received by a country and the amount of investment expenditure caused by it. Ideally one would have to make an analysis of the effects of every foreign loan. No such analysis, is, of course, possible in retrospect. It would seem that the gross import of long term capital through loans, share issues and direct investments would in most cases represent a reasonable approximation to the amount of investment caused by foreign factors. If the volume of investment had been deliberately planned by the government with an eye on its balance of payments effects, more investment could have been permitted than the equivalent of the value of the foreign capital obtained.[1] But it does not seem reasonable to interpret balance of payments planning into the history of the interwar period. Many investment projects required imports, for instance, of machinery, and part of the proceeds of a loan may have been used to finance these imports. In this respect, however, investment is not essentially different from exports, which may require the import of raw materials; and the difference in degree is one which may be disregarded (as must so many differences of degree) unless it stands out as particularly significant in a particular case.

The selection of the proper capital items from a country's balance of payments for the purpose of estimating this type of autonomous investment is not always easy. Normally the movement of outstanding securities should not be considered as a factor determining the rate of domestic investment, but rather, like short-term capital movements, as a shift in the form in which a country's foreign assets and liabilities are held. Similarly such capital import as the receipt of amortization of foreign loans would not, prima facie, be expected to produce

[1] For this "expansion ratio" see J. J. Polak, "Balance of Payments Problems of Countries Reconstructing with the Help of Foreign Loans", *Quarterly Journal of Economics*, February 1943, page 214.

additional domestic investment. Long-term loans which represent refinancing, either of other long-term or of short-term loans should, if possible, also be left out of consideration. On the other hand, some of the short-term loans of the 'twenties were considered by the borrowers, if not by the lenders, as virtually long-term loans and led to additional investment in the same way as long-term loans; to the extent possible, these loans should be included in our estimate of autonomous investment.[1]

From the various capital elements in the balance of payments of the borrowing country (or from similar statistics), an estimate can thus be made, along the lines indicated, of the value of this type of autonomous investment. The national income definition may now be written as:

$$Y = X + V_A + (C - M_c) + (V - M_v) \quad (28.1)$$

where $V$ stands for endogenous investment and $V_A$ for autonomous investment.

From this $y$ may be developed and the resulting approximation is very similar to that found before:[2]

$$v = \frac{X + V_A}{p_m} + c + v - m \quad (28 \cdot 2)$$

and hence

$$y = \frac{X + V_A}{p_m} \cdot \frac{1}{\delta + \mu} + y_o \quad (28 \cdot 3)$$

[1] It is not possible to take the total net capital movement of the balance of payments as the indicator of capital imports. For if this were added to the value of exports, one would actually arrive at the value of imports (disregarding current invisible items); $\frac{X + V_A}{p_m}$ would be identical with $\frac{M}{p_m}$ or $m$, and the measurement of the multiplier as per (22·4) would become virtually identical with the measurement of the marginal propensity to import!

[2] For countries with large capital import the assumption that $X \sim M$ used in the Annex is to be replaced, in the derivation of (22·1), by the assumption that $X + V_A \sim M$.

The difference between this equation and (24·2) is only slight: $\frac{V_A}{p_m}$ has been added to the multiplicand; the definition of the foreign factors has been expanded to

$$f = \frac{X + V_A}{p_m} \qquad (28·4)$$

Where other forms of autonomous investment, such as government deficit expenditure during certain years, appear significant compared to export fluctuations, they would be taken to the multiplicand in (28·3) after deflation, in principle, by the domestic price level, $p_d$; for practical purposes, deflation by the cost of living index, which contains also import prices, is usually a satisfactory approximation.

Reference will be made below to the role of autonomous investment (whether financed from abroad or not) in the entire system of international economic fluctuations.

## 9. AUTONOMOUS IMPORTS

An autonomous reduction in imports is equivalent in its effect on income to an autonomous increase in exports. Thus a shift in demand from imported goods to home goods—on account of a change in consumer preference or a higher tariff—will increase demand for home goods in just the same manner as an increase in exports would. It will be necessary, therefore, to make allowance for autonomous imports in our multiplicand. This is done by introducing a variable $m_A$ which, standing for autonomous *reductions* in imports, is added to $f$ in appropriate cases.

The way in which $m_A$ is measured requires a few words of explanation, in particular because the short-cut

C

expression "autonomous imports" is not in itself very clear. Within the framework of the multiplier theory, "autonomous imports" are all imports not caused by changes in income. Imports (or changes in imports) caused, say, by changes in relative prices of imported domestic goods are considered "autonomous" in this particular framework.[1] We have therefore to enter into the multiplicand as $m_A$ all the fluctuations in $m$ that are not attributable to fluctuations in $y$, with sign reversed:

$$m_A = -(m - \mu y - m_o) \qquad (29 \cdot 1)$$

Thus $m_A$ includes the allowance for other factors than income changes in the import equation, such as relative prices, or a trend; and it includes also the unexplained residual of the import equation, on the assumption that broadly speaking, this residual is due to other factors than those accounted for influencing imports, rather than to errors of measurement in the import series. The special treatment of "autonomous imports" in cases where a separate import equation was given for two sub-periods while the multiplier equation was not split, are discussed in the next chapter (Section 2).

[1] Cf. J. J. Polak, "The Foreign Trade Multiplier", *American Economic Review*, Vol. XXXVII, December 1947, p. 892, and G. Haberler's "Comment", *ibid.*, p. 901 n.

# CHAPTER III

# EXPLANATION OF THE VOLUME OF IMPORTS OF INDIVIDUAL COUNTRIES

## 1. EXPANDED IMPORT EQUATION: RELATIVE PRICES

THE import equation (21·6) assumed above implies that there is no competition between imported and home-produced commodities. To make the equation more realistic allowance has to be made for a certain influence of relative prices. The equation then becomes:

$$m = \mu y + \varepsilon \overline{m} P + m_o \qquad (31\cdot1)$$

where $P$ is the ratio of domestic over foreign prices $\left(\dfrac{p_d}{p_m}\right)$, $\varepsilon$ is the mean elasticity of substitution between domestic and foreign products, and $\overline{m}$ stands for the average value of $m$.[1] It will readily be seen that the term $\varepsilon \overline{m} P$ will have to be entered into the multiplicand if (31·1) is substituted for (21·6):

$$y = \frac{f - \varepsilon \overline{m} P}{\delta + \mu} + y_o \qquad (31\cdot2)$$

## 2. IMPORT RESTRICTIONS

Even (31·1), however, is not fully satisfactory to give a continuous explanation of the behaviour of imports in

[1] The introduction of $\overline{m}$ in the coefficient for $P$ makes $\varepsilon$ of zero dimension in $m$; $P$ itself, being a ratio of two price indices both on the same base, is already without dimension.

the interwar period in countries where severe import restrictions[1] were introduced at some time during the period covered. Often, the restrictions tended, it appears, to affect both the level and the slope of the import-income curve—both the average and the marginal propensity to import. This should, indeed, be expected: the restrictions prohibit certain categories of imports and this reduces the average level of imports; fluctuations in income can then no longer be reflected in changes in the quantities imported of these commodities; as a result the marginal propensity to import is also lowered.[2]

For the period after the introduction of restrictions we must then introduce a new equation:[3]

$$m = \mu'y + m'_o \qquad (32 \cdot 1)$$

where the accented $\mu'$, and $m'$ are different from the corresponding values in the preceding period. Graphically the relations represented by the two import equations are shown in the diagram on p. 39.

Curve I represents the relation for the period before the restrictions and curve II the restriction period.

We may indicate by $m_s$ the shift in the import curve, that is the difference, for any given rate of $y$, between $m_I$ [i.e. m according to (20·6)] and $m_{II}$ [i.e. m according to (32·1)]. If a continuous multiplier equation is used $m_s$

---

[1] Among restrictions we need not here consider tariffs, since they would be reflected in the price ratio $P$ and the reduction in imports caused by them would, therefore, be susceptible of explanation by the earlier formula. See further Section 3 below.

[2] Professor Robertson stresses the logical connection between a change in the level and a change in the marginal propensity ["Mr. Clark and the Foreign Trade Multiplier", *Econ. Journal*, Vol. XLIX (June 1939), p. 354]. There may, however, be cases where a change in the level of 10 per cent represents a very unusual break in imports, whereas a change of the propensity by the same percentage—*e.g.* from ·30 to ·27—would, with moderate fluctuations in income, hardly be noticeable.

[3] The term with $P$ has been omitted here to concentrate the argument on the particular point under discussion.

will require to be represented in the multiplicand:[1]

$$y = \frac{f + m_s}{\delta + \mu} + y_o \qquad (32\cdot2)$$

Where the shift in the import curve is parallel, $m_s$ in the above formula will be a constant. When there is both a

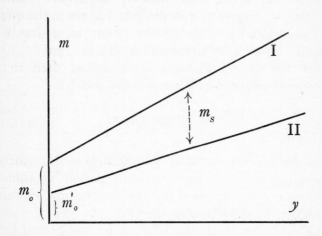

shift and a change in slope, $m_s$ will be variable and will depend on $y$:

$$m_s = (\mu - \mu')y + m_o - m'_o \qquad (32\cdot3)$$

so that the addition to the multiplicand is variable and depends on $y$. The magnitude of this term can be determined after the two import equations $(20\cdot6)$ and $(31\cdot1)$ have been fitted, yielding $\mu$, $\mu'$, $m_o$ and $m'_o$.

In practice, however, other "autonomous" factors determining imports in the second period will also have to be taken into account in the multiplicand. This can

<hr />

[1] Note that $m_s$ is defined as the *reduction* in imports in $(32\cdot3)$, hence it should be entered with a positive sign in $(32\cdot2)$.

most readily be done by combining these other influences together with $m_s$ into $m_A$, which will then be found—in graphical terms—as the distance of the actual imports from the first period import relationship, *viz*:

$$m_A = -(m - \mu y - m_0) \qquad (32 \cdot 4)$$

using $\mu$ and $m_0$ for both periods, although $\mu'$ and $m'_0$ were used in explaining imports in the second period.

This procedure implies the assumption that $\delta$ remained constant during the two periods. The multiplier for the second period, based on $\mu'$ rather than on $\mu$, is then found as follows. First $\delta$ is determined

$$\delta = \frac{1}{\text{Multiplier of first period}} - \mu \qquad (32 \cdot 5)$$

and then:

$$\text{Multiplier of second period} = \frac{1}{\delta + \mu'}, \qquad (32 \cdot 6)$$

## 3. IMPORT RESTRICTIONS AND RELATIVE PRICES

A special word of explanation is required to justify the statement that shifts in the import curve as a result of import restrictions cannot be explained by reference to relative prices. One might expect that, if imports were restricted, consumers would bid up the prices of imported goods to a level where they would bear such a relationship to the prices of domestic goods that the reduced demand for imported goods at the higher relative price could just be satisfied from the quantities which the government allows to be imported. If that were so, and $P$ reflected the actual price ratio, why then could the volume of imports not be explained by $(31 \cdot 1)$?

There are two reasons why $(31 \cdot 1)$ does not give a satisfactory explanation. The first is that, in almost all cases, the price index of imported commodities which we use reflects the unit value of imports, not their internal wholesale price; it reflects the price paid by the importer, not the price paid by the ultimate consumer or user, and therefore does not reflect the increased scarcity profits of the importers. The second reason is that import restrictions are normally applied in order to stimulate home production of substitutes, *i.e.* they are applied to the commodities with the very highest elasticity of substitution. An elasticity of substitution $\varepsilon$ derived on the basis of the price-quantity movement of all imported commodities in the 'twenties may therefore be quite inadequate to explain the price-quantity movement of the section of imported commodities to which restrictions are applied.

Both reasons, it will be observed, are purely statistical in nature. Given the index numbers of prices at our disposal, we require the equations of Section 2 above to explain the past. But we need not incorporate these equations in our system. Logically (31·1) should suffice to explain imports, provided $P$ is based on the proper price indices and $\varepsilon$ measures the true price elasticity. In the theoretical part, we shall, therefore, proceed on this basis, without any further reference to $m_s$.

## 4. THE INTERNATIONAL REFLECTION RATIO

We may summarize the steps we have taken. We have, in Chapter II, established the relation between foreign factors and national income. In this chapter we have established the relation between national income and imports. We may now, by combining the two steps and eliminating $y$ from (31·1) and (31·2) establish the relation between the foreign factors and imports (omitting $v_A$ and a constant term):

$$m = \frac{\mu}{\delta + \mu} (f - \varepsilon \bar{m} P) + \varepsilon \bar{m} P \qquad (34 \cdot 1)$$

We may first consider this relation under the simplifying assumptions that relative prices are constant and that there is no foreign lending: $(p_m = p_x, P = 1, f = x)$. This reduces (34·1) to:

$$m = \frac{\mu}{\delta + \mu} \cdot x \qquad (34\cdot2)$$

The fraction $\dfrac{\mu}{\delta + \mu}$ indicates the ratio between a change in the volume of exports and the ensuing change in the volume of imports; it indicates, in other words, the intensity with which the country under consideration reflects back into the world impulses it receives from the rest of the world. We shall call this ratio the "*international reflection ratio*" and indicate it by $\rho$:

$$\rho = \frac{\mu}{\delta + \mu} \qquad (34\cdot3)$$

It follows from our definition that $\rho \gtreqless 1$ according as to $\delta \lesseqgtr 0$. The two values, $\rho = 1$, $\delta = 0$, are both critical values for the stability of the country's economy. If $\delta = 0$, the multiplier would be infinite but for the fact that part of the domestic impetus is passed to foreign countries through imports; the economy of the country is stable only owing to the stability of other economies. Similarly if $\rho = 1$, the country passes back with equal intensity any impetus it receives from abroad. If the economic system of the world as a whole is stable, it must be because in a sufficient number of other countries $\rho < 1$.

## 5. FURTHER DISCUSSION OF THE INTERNATIONAL REFLECTION RATIO

A short digression on the concept of the reflection ratio, which involves at the same time a certain widening of the concept, may perhaps be useful. So far this ratio has been described entirely as an effect operating through the income of the economy under study. But we may well expand it to cover also responses of the government of the country to changes in its reserve position.

If the value of exports increases by $\triangle X$, and the private reflection ratio relating to income responses through the private sector only, is $\rho_P$, then imports will rise by:

$$\triangle M = \rho_P \triangle X \qquad (35\cdot1)$$

If the balance of payments was in equilibrium before, reserves $(R)$ will increase by the difference:[1]

$$\triangle R = \triangle X - \triangle M = (1 - \rho_P)\triangle X \qquad (35\cdot2)$$

which will be positive if $\rho_P < 1$.

Here $\triangle R$ is the rate of increase of reserves per unit of time which will gradually be approached as long as the higher level of exports $X + \triangle X$ continues and as, over successive periods, imports increase to the rate of $M + \rho_P \triangle X$. Initially, before the effect of the greater exports has worked itself out fully on income and imports, the rate of increase in reserves will be greater.

The improvement in the reserve position is likely to set in motion two types of responses of the government, especially in those countries where the pressure towards capital expenditure for development is strong. First, the government will be inclined to allow a certain increase in credit expansion by relaxing restrictive policies such as bank reserve requirements or credit control, or by extending its own borrowing for development purposes. Secondly, where imports are restricted, the government is likely to relax these restrictions. As a result, imports

---

[1] Assuming all items in the balance of payments to be subsumed under exports, imports and changes in reserves.

will further increase and may reach the point where they again equal exports. By these actions of the government, the total reflection ratio of the country will then just have been raised to unity.

If the private reflection ratio is itself close to unity, there will of course be little room for such relaxation by the government, provided always that the government bases its action on the ultimate value for $\triangle R$, and not on the higher value which will appear in the first few months or quarters. Should the government relax its internal or import controls (without other offsetting measures) in a way just calculated to absorb the initial increases in reserves, it will find itself losing reserves by the time the full effects of $\triangle X$ on imports are showing themselves; and at least a partial reversal of the policy changes will then appear necessary.[1]

## 6. THE TOTAL EFFECT OF CHANGES IN RELATIVE PRICES ON IMPORTS

Introducing now relative prices, we may rewrite (34·1) with the help of $\rho$:

$$m = \rho x + (1 - \rho)\, \varepsilon \overline{m} P \qquad (36·1)$$

or

$$m = \rho \frac{X}{p_m} + (1 - \rho)\, \varepsilon \overline{m} \frac{p_d}{p_m} \qquad (36·2)$$

From this we can derive the total effect (*i.e.* sum of the direct effect plus the effect *via* income) of changes in $p_d$ and $p_m$. It will be seen that both depend very much on $\rho$. If $\rho = 1, \dfrac{dm}{dp_d} = 0$, independently of the value of $\varepsilon$: an increase in imports caused by an increase in domestic

---

[1] A similar case where expansion based on foreign capital might easily overshoot the mark is discussed in J. J. Polak, "Balance of Payments Problems . . .", *Quarterly Journal of Economics*, February 1943, pp. 214–16.

prices (with foreign prices constant) ultimately reduces income by the same amount as the reduction in imports; and since there is no internal damping, the full effect of this fall in income is reflected in a reduction of imports of equal size, which thus fully offsets the initial increase of imports.

The effect of changes in $p_m$ is more complicated, since they affect also the first term on the right-hand side of (36·2). We find, selecting arbitrarily the base of both index numbers $p_m$ and $p_d$ as 1 at the point of differentiation:

$$\frac{dm}{dp_m} = - [\rho X + (1 - \rho) \varepsilon \overline{m}] \quad (36 \cdot 3)$$

or, using the approximation $X = \overline{m}$,

$$\frac{dm}{dp_m} = \overline{m} [\rho + (1 - \rho) \varepsilon] \quad (36 \cdot 4)$$

The form between [ ] on the right-hand side of (36·4) indicates the "total elasticity" of imports with respect to import prices, if export prices are kept constant. For $\rho = 1$, this total elasticity becomes:

$$\frac{dm}{\overline{m}} \cdot \frac{p_m}{dp_m} = 1 \quad (36 \cdot 5)$$

If $\rho$ is near unity (*e.g.* $\rho = 0·8$), the value of the total elasticity depends only to a minor extent on $\varepsilon$; in fact for most values of $\varepsilon$ it will be quite near to unity (*e.g.* for $\rho = 0·8$, $\varepsilon = 0·5$, the elasticity will be $0·9$; for the same value of $\rho$ but $\varepsilon = 1·5$, it will be $1·1$). This finding can also be put as follows: if $\delta$ is close to 0 and hence $\rho$ close to 1, the main effect of a fall in import prices on imports is *via* an increase in real incomes. The fall in import prices also leads to an increase in imports by substitution for domestic products. But this effect on imports is for a good deal offset by the fall in income it entails, which in turn leads to a reduction of imports.

## 7. DIRECT DETERMINATION OF THE INTERNATIONAL REFLECTION RATIO

For countries for which no national income series exists, (36·2) may be used to determine $\rho$ directly. If a high value for $\rho$ is found, it is likely that no significant influence of $\frac{p_d}{p_m}$ will be found. This, then, does not indicate much about the value of $\varepsilon$; it only shows that the product $(1 - \rho)\varepsilon$ is very small. From the value found for $\rho$, one can derive the value for $\delta$ and for the multiplier, provided an estimate can be made for $\mu$, for instance on the basis of some knowledge concerning the average propensity to import.

# CHAPTER IV

# EXPLANATION OF THE VOLUME OF EXPORTS OF INDIVIDUAL COUNTRIES

## 1. EXPORTS AS THE MAIN FOREIGN FACTOR

THE factor $f$ which we have used to describe the elements "foreign" to any one economy under consideration consists of various components: the volume of exports $(x)$; export prices $(p_x)$ and import prices $(p_m)$; and, for some countries, foreign loans. For reasons discussed below,[1] fluctuations in the terms of trade $\frac{p_x}{p_m}$ are of secondary importance for the system as a whole; and we consider the volume of foreign loans as determined, to a considerable extent, by extra-economic factors. The main factor, therefore, to be explained here is the volume of exports.

## 2. THE PROBLEM OF AGGREGATION: USE OF WORLD TRADE

In a sense, this is not a new problem, since we have already explained the volume of imports for all countries. But in considering all the flows of trade from any one country to any other from the point of view of exports, another aggregation of these flows is required than when considering them from the point of view of imports. If $t_{ij}$ be the trade from country $i$ to country $j$ (where $i, j = 1, 2 \ldots \ldots n$; $i \neq j$) then the total imports and exports

[1] *Cf.* page 58.

of country $k$ ($m_k$ and $x_k$) are aggregated as follows:

$$m_k = \Sigma_i t_{ik} \ (i = 1, 2, \ldots \ldots n; i \neq k) \qquad (42 \cdot 1)$$

and $\qquad x_k = \Sigma_j t_{kj} \ (j = 1, 2 \ldots \ldots n; j \neq k) \qquad (42 \cdot 2)$

Ideally, one would want to explain every one element $t_{ij}$ of world trade. But in practice this is not possible, at least not for a first approximation, and we have to use some reasonable procedure of aggregation.

Omitting, provisionally, fluctuations in relative prices, we have

$$t_{ij} = \mu_{ij} y_j \qquad (i, j = 1, 2 \ldots n; i \neq j) \qquad (42 \cdot 3)$$

where $\mu_{ij}$ is the marginal propensity of country $j$ to import from country $i$. The variables $t$ and $y$ are expressed in comparable units, e.g. in millions of dollars at constant prices. The export of country $k$ then is, as per $(42 \cdot 2)$:

$$x_k = \Sigma_j t_{kj} = \Sigma_j \mu_{kj} y_j \ (j = 1, 2 \ldots n; j \neq k) \qquad (42 \cdot 4)$$

Now we may decompose $\mu_{kj}$ into two systematic elements:

$$\mu_{kj} = \mu_j \sigma_k \qquad\qquad (42 \cdot 5)$$

where $\mu_j$ : is the general marginal propensity to import of country $j$, reflecting the size, specialization, etc., of that country; and

$\qquad \sigma_k$ : is the marginal relative importance of country $k$ in world trade.

A third element, reflecting the degree of economic, political or geographical affinity between country $k$ and country $j$ can, unfortunately, not be allowed for in our method of aggregation. This element would indicate that where this affinity is strong, $\mu_{kj}$ is greater than as expressed by $(42 \cdot 5)$; while, where it is weak, $\mu_{kj}$ is smaller.

Since $\sigma_k$ is the same for all values of $j$, we may now write $(42\cdot4)$:

$$x_k = \sigma_k \Sigma_j \mu_j y_j \quad (j = 1, 2 \ldots n; j \neq k) \quad (42\cdot6)$$

or

$$x_k = \sigma_k \Sigma_j m_j \quad\quad\quad\quad\quad\quad\quad (42\cdot7)$$

Since for the world as a whole, $\Sigma m = \Sigma x = x_w$

$$x_k = \sigma_k [x_w - m_k] \quad\quad\quad\quad (42\cdot8)$$

and, using $(34\cdot2)$:

$$x_k = \frac{\sigma_k}{1 + \rho_k \sigma_k} x_w \quad\quad (42\cdot9)$$

For countries having only a small percentage of world trade, both in the average and marginally, this adjustment of world trade on account of the imports of the country under consideration is a matter of very secondary importance. We introduce, for convenience:

$$\sigma'_k = \frac{\sigma_k}{1 + \rho_k \sigma_k} \quad\quad (42\cdot10)$$

In the sections dealing with individual countries $x_k$ and $x_w$ are expressed as index numbers with the same base period, rather than in dollars at constant prices. We use $\xi_k$ to indicate the relationship between $x_k$ and $x_w$ expressed as index numbers.

$$x_k = \xi_k x_w \quad\quad\quad\quad (42\cdot11)$$

where $\xi_k = \dfrac{\sigma'_k}{\text{share of country } k \text{ in world trade}} \quad (42\cdot12)$

# 3. ALTERNATIVE AGGREGATION: USE OF WORLD INCOME

It follows from (42·11) that the relation between the exports of any one country and income in other countries can be found by correlating its exports with the volume of world trade. Other authors, following, probably, the analogy of the import equation of one country, have tried to explain one country's exports on the basis of world income.[1] This procedure is, however, less satisfactory for two reasons. In the first place, it fails to make allowance not only, like our method, for the third element mentioned above, but also for differences in the $\mu$'s, unless the $y$'s actually move parallel. Thus an increase in income of $100 million in the United States, where the marginal propensity to import is very low, is given the same weight as an increase of the same absolute magnitude in the United Kingdom, whose propensity to import is much higher.[2]

In the second place, comparison of one country's exports with world trade, rather than world income, is preferable because it is not affected by any general shift in the income-import relationship of the other countries. If there is a residual $\mu_j$ in the import equation of country $j$:

$$m_j = \mu_j y_j + u_j \qquad (43·1)$$

[1] Randall Hinshaw and Lloyd A. Metzler, "World Prosperity and the British Balance of Payments", *Review of Economic Statistics* (XXVII), November 1945, pages 156–170.

T. C. Chang, "The British Balance of Payments, 1924–38", *The Economic Journal*, December 1947.

J. Tinbergen, "Some Remarks on the Problem of Dollar Scarcity", *Proceedings of the International Statistical Conferences* (Washington, September 6–18, 1947), Vol. V, pages 73–97.

[2] Probably in order to eliminate extreme effects of the omission of the $\mu$'s, Hinshaw and Metzler calculate the world national income exclusive of the U.S.S.R. (*op. cit.*, Table A–2).

and if this is general for all the countries from which country $j$ imports so that:

$$u_{kj} = \sigma_k u \qquad (43\cdot2)$$

then $(42\cdot6)$ becomes:

$$x_k = \sigma_k \Sigma_j \left( \mu_j y_j + u_j \right) \qquad (43\cdot3)$$

but $(42\cdot7)$ remains unchanged.

Thus the imposition of import controls in the 'thirties, reducing imports compared to national income, does not invalidate the explanation of exports of any one country if the explanatory variable is world trade (provided the country under consideration has been affected by the restrictions roughly as much as other countries); but when world income is used as the explanatory variable, a large residual appears.[1]

## 4. EXPANDED EXPORT EQUATION: RELATIVE PRICES

In addition to income abroad, relative price may be an important factor determining a country's exports. The effect of this factor may be considered in two steps. First, the ratio between the price level of any importing country $j$ and an average of the price levels in the rest of the world (in which the weight of the prices in any one exporting country $k$ is small) determines the magnitude of $m_j$. Secondly, the share which falls to country $k$ in the actual volume of imports of all countries $j$ depends on the ratio of prices in country $k$ to prices in the world (in world prices, in turn, prices in each individual country $j$ have a small weight).

[1] This residual was taken care of by Tinbergen in his explanation of U.S. exports by using as an additional explanatory variable an "index of trade barriers" (*op. cit.*, p. 92).

D

To take the second step into consideration we insert a relative price term into $(42\cdot11)$ and write

$$x_k = \xi_k x_w + 100\eta_k\frac{p_k}{p_w} \qquad (44\cdot1)$$

where    $\eta_k$ : the export elasticity[1]

$p_w$ : an appropriate price index of world trade

$x_k$ and $x_w$ : indices of the country's exports and of world trade whose average over the period is taken as 100.

In the special case where $\xi_k = 1$, and assuming that there is zero correlation between $x_w$ and $\frac{p_k}{p_w}$, $(44\cdot1)$ reduces to

$$\frac{x_k}{x_w} = 1 + \eta_k\frac{p_k}{p_w} \qquad (44\cdot2)$$

This is the formula used by Tinbergen[2] to measure $\eta_k$; it is clear that this formula is legitimate only if the special condition $\xi_k = 1$ is fulfilled, or, in economic terms, if the margninal propensity of the world to buy from country $k$ equals the average propensity to buy from country $k$. For a number of countries our figures for $\xi_k$ bear out this fact; for others, however, $\xi_k$ is quite different from unity and a significant increase in correlation, as well as a more accurate measurement of $\xi_k$, is found if $x_w$ is used as a separate explanatory variable, rather than combined with $x_k$ in a fixed 1 : 1 ratio.[3]

[1] Tinbergen introduces an "elasticity of substitution" and a "quota elasticity" for exports, which are equal if standard index numbers are used ("Some Measurements of Elasticities of Substitution", *Review of Economic Statistics*, XXVIII, No. 3, August 1946, page 110). On the assumption that $x_w$ does not change as $\frac{p_k}{p_w}$ changes, our $\eta$ would be equal to the quota elasticity.

[2] Source as in preceding footnote.

[3] For further comment on the bias which Tinbergen's figures contain, *cf.* J. J. Polak, "Note on the Measurement of Elasticity of Substitution in International Trade", *Review of Economics and Statistics*, Vol. XXXII, No. 1, February 1950, pages 16–20.

# CHAPTER V

# THE INTERNATIONAL ECONOMIC SYSTEM

## 1. THE ENDOGENOUS SYSTEM

THE three preceding chapters indicated the position of an individual country in world trade. It is necessary, now, to combine the relationships concerning individual countries into one set of equations describing the world economy. In doing so, we may conveniently distinguish between what are, in this world system, endogenous and exogenous variables. For the world as a whole we consider as endogenous the exports $(x)$, national income $(y)$, and imports $(m)$ of each country. We consider as exogenous, on the other hand, certain other variables which have been introduced at various places in the preceding chapters, such as autonomous investment $(v_A)$ and price ratios $\left(\dfrac{p_d}{p_m}, \dfrac{p_x}{p_w}\right)$.

The network of the relations between the endogenous variables may be said to represent the international economic system—the given framework through which successive waves of shocks are communicated from one country to another. The exogenous variables are these shocks which keep the system in motion.

In order to concentrate first on the endogenous, systematic, part of the system, we write for each country the relations explaining its exports, national income and imports, omitting all exogenous variables and constant terms. We use the subscript $i$ to distinguish the various

countries. All variables are in billions of dollars at
constant prices.

$$x_i = \sigma'_i x_w \qquad (51 \cdot 1)$$

$$y_i = \frac{x_i}{\delta_i + \mu_i} \qquad (51 \cdot 2)$$

$$m_i = \mu_i y_i \qquad (51 \cdot 3)$$

In these equations $\sigma'_i$, $\delta_i$ and $\mu_i$ represent certain
coefficients which have been derived in the previous
chapters; $x_w$ stands for the volume of world trade.

With the help of the international reflection ratio $\rho_i$
as defined in $(34 \cdot 3)$ we can immediately combine these
three equations into one:

$$m_i = \rho_i \sigma'_i x_w + a_i \qquad (51 \cdot 4)$$

In this one equation we introduce $a_i$ for the total effect
upon imports of all exogenous variables which have been
omitted from $(51 \cdot 1)$, $(51 \cdot 2)$ and $(51 \cdot 3)$.

By summing $(51 \cdot 4)$ from all countries we obtain

$$\Sigma_i m_i = x_w \Sigma \rho_i \sigma'_i + \Sigma_i a_i \qquad (51 \cdot 5)$$

and since $\Sigma_i m_i = x_w$, $(51 \cdot 5)$ can be simplified to

$$x_w = \frac{A}{1 - \Sigma_i \rho_i \sigma'_i} \qquad (51 \cdot 6)$$

where $\qquad A = \Sigma_i a_i$

The systematic part of this equation is represented by
the term $\dfrac{1}{1 - \Sigma_i \rho_i \sigma'_i}$, which represents a "world multiplier"; the autonomous shocks are represented by $A$, the
aggregate of the exogenous variables measured by the

extent to which each of them increases directly the imports of the country in which it occurs.

It will be readily seen that the expression $\Sigma_i \rho_i \sigma'_i$ stands for a weighted average of the $\rho_i$'s of the individual countries, with the $\sigma_i$'s (the "marginal propensities of the world to import from country $i$") as the weights. It is probable *a priori* that the $\rho$'s will normally be $<1$. Accordingly their weighted average will also be $<1$; and the system described by (51·6) will be damped. We shall find, in fact, that the damping is rather great, so that the value of $x_w$ will adjust itself rather rapidly to $A$, the net sum of the shocks operating in the system.

## 2. TWO CATEGORIES OF SHOCKS

We must now pay further attention to the nature of these shocks. Two categories of shocks may be distinguished. The first, of which autonomous investment is the most prominent example, adds to the import of one country without simultaneously reducing imports of another country. The other type of shock is primarily redistributive in its effect: it adds to the imports of one country but simultaneously reduces the imports of one or more other countries. The addition and the subtraction need not be exactly equal and the net effect of the redistribution of the volume of total world trade need not, therefore, be precisely zero. Nevertheless, compared to the effects on aggregate world trade of the first type of shocks, those of the second type are of a second order of magnitude.

## 3. AUTONOMOUS INVESTMENT

Our computations made for individual countries show many instances of important deviations of actual real national income from the values computed on the basis of the foreign factors. Apart from inaccuracies in the statistical material, these deviations represent autonomous fluctuations in national income, due, it would be expected, usually to autonomous fluctuations in domestic investment. These fluctuations may either reflect autonomous private investment or autonomous[1] changes in the magnitude of the government surplus or deficit. Abrupt changes in financial policy, or unusual expenditure for military preparations are typical of factors which may cause autonomous changes in "investment" and thereby in imports. Private investment may show autonomous changes as a result of sudden changes of business expectations (as a result, for instance, of changed political conditions), new discoveries or inventions, changes in the rate of interest due to the introduction of new governmental policies in this field, strikes and many other causes not directly reflecting current business conditions.

Autonomous factors may make themselves felt in any country. There is no country where the export-national income relationship would show no residual in any year or where all imperfection in the correlation could be ascribed to imperfections in the statistical data. But in the general picture of world trade as a whole autonomous changes in large and rich countries are likely to play a much more important role than those in small and poor countries. There are three reasons for this.

(i) Large countries normally export a smaller proportion of their total production than small countries.[2] Accordingly, the relative effect on their national income of a same percentage fluctuation in their exports is

[1] Such changes in the government's financial position which are part of the normal cyclical pattern are not considered autonomous in this connection.

[2] *Cf.* T. C. Chang, "International Comparison of Demand for Imports", *Review of Economic Studies*, 1945–46, XIII (2), pages 53–67. Mr. Chang's categories I, II, and III (pages 55–6) refer mainly to countries of different size. His figures refer to the ratio of imports to national income; this ratio is highly correlated with that of exports to total national production.

smaller for large, than for small, countries, and the relative significance of autonomous fluctuations is, therefore, greater.

(ii) Autonomous movements which by their nature affect a whole country are likely to be of larger absolute importance in large countries than in small countries, and are therefore less likely to be cancelled out by simultaneous autonomous movements in other countries: a railroad strike or cheap money policy in a large country will affect world income and world trade[1] more than similar occurrences in small countries.

(iii) Finally, large and in particular rich, countries will more readily have the reserves, both domestic and foreign, to afford autonomous developments, whether private or governmental. A small, poor country may have a sudden strong tendency towards an investment boom or a public works policy—but a great proportion of the investment goods required or of the consumer goods purchased by the additional income paid out will have to come from abroad, and if the country's foreign exchange resources are small, the boom will almost inevitably subside before long.

Therefore, although logically in our system autonomous movements can and do occur in any and all countries of the system, in practice those movements are by far the most important in the few large and rich countries of the world. Among these the United States stands out on account of one additional characteristic, which we may perhaps call the volatility of its economy. Periods of optimism and pessimism, of boom and bear speculation, alternate with more intensity in the United States than in most other countries. At least in the interwar period, prices and wages were more flexible in the

[1] This statement implies that the propensity to import falls less than in proportion to size. It is obvious that this is the case from the fact that generally countries with larger income also have larger trade.

United States than in other highly industrialized countries. The factors of size, reserves and volatility combined
make the United States the dominant, though by no
means the sole, origin of autonomous changes in investment in the world economy.

## 4 . IMPORT RESTRICTIONS

Import restrictions also constituted an import category of autonomous shocks, all in a downward direction,
in the volume of world trade. The magnitude of the initial restriction did not, however, determine its impact on
the volume of imports of the country applying the restriction. Any restriction of imports *by category* led to an
increase in other imports which would go a considerable
distance towards offsetting the original restriction; the
net effect of such restrictions would bear a ratio of $(1 - \rho)$
to the original restriction. In many countries the effect
of import restrictions may have been much more to increase income at a given level of imports than actually to
restrict the volume of imports itself.

## 5 . CHANGES IN RELATIVE PRICES

Changes in relative prices, both on the export and on
the import side, constitute autonomous influences for the
countries from which, or to which, demand is shifted as a
result of them. But they are of much less significance for
total world trade. Thus, if a country depreciates (or de-
flates) and thus increases its exports, its national income
and hence its imports will rise.[1] But at the same time the
exports of one or more competing countries will fall by
exactly the same amount, assuming that other factors do
not change the total volume of world trade. Their

[1] This is only one part of the chain of causation. Imports will tend to fall on
account of the substitution of domestic for foreign products as the former become
relatively cheaper.

national incomes and hence their imports will decline. The net result will depend on the precise values of the $\rho$'s for the countries concerned. According to (36·1) a given shift in exports of $x_0$ from country 1 to country 2 will reduce $m_1$ by $\rho_1 x_0$ and increase $m_2$ by $\rho_2 x_0$. The net autonomous impact on the volume of world trade will thus be $x_0(\rho_2 - \rho_1)$. Without information concerning the two $\rho$'s it cannot be known whether the effect is positive or negative. In general, however, it may be stated that shifts of trade from any one country to any other country, be it by depreciation, export subsidies, discrimination in imports, or whatever measures, have only a second order effect on the volume of world trade, the sign of which is uncertain.[1]

In certain specified conditions one should expect the effect of a shift to be to increase world production, though not necessarily at the same time world trade. This would be so in particular if country 2 has large unused capacity and expansion of production and real national income is, therefore, possible in that country, whilst country 1 has full employment and is in or near inflation. In such a situation the transfer, by a third country, of exports from 1 to 2 will probably increase the volume of world activity. Country 2 might have come into the position sketched as a result of domestic inflation, which would have raised its prices above competitive levels. Depreciation of the currency of country 2 would then tend to increase world activity.

Depreciation of one currency may increase the volume of world trade in another somewhat special case, viz. if the resulting improvement in the balance of payments of the depreciating country induces it to relax its

[1] This view is opposite to that maintained by Professor Frisch. See Ragnar Frisch, "On the Need for Forecasting a Mutilateral Balance of Payments", American Economic Review, Vol. XXXVII (September 1947), pages 531–51, and J. J. Polak, "Balancing International Trade: A Comment on Professor Frisch's Paper", American Economic Review, Vol. XXXVIII (March 1948), pages 139–42.

import restrictions to a point where its imports increase
by more than the amount corresponding to the rise in
exports, while the deterioration in the balance of payments of other countries does not induce the latter to
impose equivalent import restrictions. In general, however, there is no ground for the presumption that the
depreciation of a currency will increase the volume of
world trade—except for the, normally minor, ex-
pansionary effects exercised by depreciation *via* gold
production, gold holdings, and the legal reserve position
of central banks.

# CHAPTER VI

# GENERAL STATISTICAL OBSERVATIONS

## 1. INTRODUCTION

OUR purpose is to bring to actual life the theoretical structure developed in Chapters II to V by applying it to the statistical data for the interwar period. We apply it to as many countries as we can, using all available statistical data. The width of coverage thus obtained is useful for various purposes. In the first place, if the theoretical coefficients are worth knowing for one country, they are worth knowing for any country for which they can be found. Secondly, since our system is a "world system", coefficients for as nearly as possible all countries are required in order to make it reasonably complete. Thirdly, the attempt to apply the theory to the data of countries with widely different economic conditions may bring out sharply for only a few countries (perhaps only for one) an interesting complication which would deserve consideration in the case of all countries. And, finally, since many of the coefficients are, inevitably, imprecise, more confidence can be had in the general order of magnitude of the values found for many countries than in the actual values found for a few. One of the main results of our measurements, the damping of the world system, represents a weighted average of all $\rho$'s and is, therefore, relatively less uncertain than the individual $\rho$'s which make up the average.

## 2. THE CORRELATION TECHNIQUE

In order to find quantitative values for the various

coefficients we use the technique of correlation, both simple and multiple. The application of this technique to economic data has always been the subject of a good deal of suspicion on the part of many[1] and certain specific weaknesses have recently been brought to light by the work of the Cowles Commission group at the University of Chicago.[2] It appears, however, that the consequences of these weaknesses are not too serious for the type of measurements made in this study.[3] It is obvious that the relations described can neither be expected to be exactly constant over any long period of time, nor to provide a complete explanation of the phenomenon which they intend to explain. The measurements of coefficients will therefore, inevitably, yield results that are beset by a considerable margin of uncertainty. Accordingly, correlation methods cannot yield, in this field, more than a general indication of the orders of magnitude of the coefficients involved. In such a situation alternative methods of computation, even if they increased somewhat the precision of our estimates of the coefficients, would appear to be of relatively minor importance.

The reader should realize, also, that the coefficients found for individual countries do not result from automatic application of the theoretical equations to given sets of statistical data on the basis of which every research

[1] Lord Keynes's views may be referred to in this connection. "The Statistical Testing of Business Cycle Theories", *Economic Journal*, Vol. 49, September 1939.

[2] T. Haavelmo, "The Statistical Implications of a System of Simultaneous Equations", *Econometrica*, Vol. II, 1943, pages 1–12.

T. Koopmans, "Statistical Estimation of Simultaneous Economic Relations", Cowles Commission Paper, No. 11.

[3] Mention may be made of a recent paper in which it is shown that "the Haavelmo bias (attributed to the fitting by the least square method of individual relations out of a total system) is not present when we are dealing with simultaneous equations of the sequence analysis type". (R. Bentzel and H. Wold, "On statistical demand analysis from the viewpoint of simultaneous equations", *Skandinavisk Aktuarietidskrift*, 1946, 1–2, pages 95–114; quotation from page 96.) The three successive causal equations fitted for each country would seem to satisfy the authors' conditions of being "recursive" and, if so, may properly be fitted individually by the least squares method.

worker who accepted the same theory would have to arrive at the same coefficients. These coefficients involve, rather, a considerable amount of trial and error and the application of knowledge (or "impression") derived from other sources concerning the magnitude of certain coefficients. Considerable freedom was left to introduce relative prices or not; to introduce trend terms; to make allowance for capital imports and to choose a plausible series representing them; to break the period into two parts for the import equation; or to introduce special variables. Initial calculations yielding multipliers of less than about 1·25 were rejected except where it seemed plausible that the origin of the low figure was with the national income statistics and the excessively low multiplier was matched by an excessively high marginal propensity to import. Cases of improbably high multipliers or elasticities were also subjected to further scrutiny. Instances of low correlation were made the occasion for further study into the particulars of the economy of the country and in the statistics used. In all cases, the pattern of residuals was analysed for possible suggestions. To some, this procedure may appear as unpermissible "doctoring": "doctoring" of the figures to agree with the theory and "doctoring" of the theory to agree with the figures. More generously, and it is hoped, more accurately, the method may be described as an attempt to make an integrated analytical description of actual economic events on the basis of the total knowledge available —theoretical knowledge, statistical knowledge, and general descriptive information.

## 3. THE NEED FOR SHORT CUTS

The system of equations for individual countries has been written out with different degrees of completeness at various stages in the preceding chapters. The chains which constitute the link between the incoming foreign factors (exports, etc.) on the one hand, and imports on the other hand, can be indicated in greater or less detail. For the best statistical measurement of the entire concatenation, it would be desirable to use, in all countries, the statistical information concerning all economic variables which play some role in this process. In practice this would amount to fitting statistically for each country a large system of equations involving perhaps thirty to fifty variables. This would clearly be unmanageable. If this degree of differentiation is dropped, there is also no point in relating consumption and investment separately to national income, as in $(21 \cdot 5)$ and $(24 \cdot 1)$, since the two explanations would run exactly parallel and only the sum of the two coefficients found $(\varphi + \gamma)$ would be used. Reliable investment statistics are, moreover, usually not available for the interwar period even where data on national income exist. For both reasons we measure the multiplier directly. In those instances where national income data are either non-existent or so unreliable as to make their use for our purposes inadvisable, a further and final step was taken and imports were correlated directly with the foreign factor $f$.[1]

## 4. RELIABILITY OF COEFFICIENTS

Not all coefficients found have the same degree of reliability. As a general rule it is found that the "income coefficients" ($\xi$, the multiplier, and $\mu$) are much more reliable than the coefficients indicating the effects of changes in relative prices. The influence of changes in relative prices in the total fluctuations in the interwar

[1] If our primary purpose had been to determine the separate coefficients $\delta$ and $\mu$, correlation of $y$ with exports and of imports with $y$ would have been indicated, however weak the $y$ series. But since we are primarily interested in the combined coefficient $\rho$, two separate correlations with an unreliable intermediate series may have no other effect than to worsen our estimate of this coefficient.

period appears to have been rather minor. The pattern of trade and income in most countries was, on the whole, one of parallel increase and decrease much more than of shifts in favour of one country at the expense of another.[1] The price indices which had to be used are, moreover, not particularly suitable to bring into sharp focus those particular movements of relative prices which may be most significant in affecting the relative share of world trade which a country will receive, or the competitive position between imported and domestic products. The weakness of many of the price coefficients found must be acknowledged; so must the uncertainty in the instances where no significant price coefficients could be found. This fact limits the usefulness of the study in this particular respect. Conclusions on the effects of changes of relative prices and hence also as to the effects of exchange rate policy cannot safely be drawn from the data presented. Another type of analysis, more directly geared to measuring price effects, will, if possible, have to be devised to measure the relevant price coefficients with sufficient accuracy. Yet it is useful to take prices into consideration in the correlations, even though the price coefficients found are of dubious significance. The price variables perform at least the function of what might be called "cleaning variables"—that is to say, they absorb, as well as possible, whatever price effects are reflected in the material and thus help to minimize the influence of these effects on the income coefficients. Thus the role of the price variables is very similar to that of the trend in many other correlations: the trend absorbs the effects of certain long-term tendencies or certain gradually increasing errors in the main series that are correlated, but the actual trend coefficient found is not considered to have any particular meaning.

[1] The movements of exports of primary products for some countries are an important exception.

Fortunately, the deficiency of the price coefficients is not of great consequence for the system as a whole, since price factors affect primarily the parts, rather than the total. As mentioned in the preceding chapter, the effects of price changes are primarily redistributive in nature, with only second order effects on the total volume of trade. Our inability to find reliable price coefficients does, therefore, not greatly affect our ability to derive a picture of the endogenous working of the system as a whole.

The relative price series used in the explanation of the exports of various countries producing agricultural products proved inadequate to provide the explanation desired; in some of these cases the use of an index of total agricultural production ($h$ = harvest) yielded better results; in such cases this exogenous variable was used.

## 5. THE INDETERMINACY OF PROPENSITIES

The numerical values for the coefficients found by correlation may be expressed either in absolute or in relative terms. In the latter form they are usually called "elasticities", whereas some coefficients in the former form are called "propensities". The relation between the two equals the ratio of the absolute values of the two variables compared.[1] For the purpose of our system of linear equations it is necessary to work primarily with absolute coefficients rather than elasticities. This, combined with the fact that our variables are expressed in real terms, i.e. "at constant prices", has the curious effect

[1] If one assumes constant elasticity, the correlation has to be made on the basis of the logarithms of the variables. The result of a correlation based on the absolute values of the variables can, however, also serve to measure the elasticity of the relationship. This elasticity will then, however, not be constant but will depend in each point on the ratio between the variables. Often an average elasticity computed on the basis of the average ratio of the two variables will be a satisfactory measure.

of rendering the coefficients to some extent indeterminate. The problem may be made clear by an example. In a certain country the domestic price level remains constant during a depression, while the prices of its imports are halved.

The following figures show its national income and imports in 1929 and 1933, expressed at prices of the two years respectively:

| | At 1929 *prices* | | At 1933 *prices* | |
| | *National Income* | *Volume of Imports* | *National Income* | *Volume of Imports* |
| *Year* | | | | |
|---|---|---|---|---|
| 1929 | 100 | 20 | 100 | 10 |
| 1933 | 90 | 18 | 90 | 9 |
| Absolute Decline | 10 | 2 | 10 | 1 |
| Percentage Decline | 10 | 10 | 10 | 10 |
| Marginal Propensity to import | | ·20 | | ·10 |
| Income Elasticity of imports | | 1·00 | | 1·00 |

Since imports expressed in 1933 prices are a much smaller proportion of national income than expressed in 1929 prices, the propensity relating a given change in the volume of imports to a given change in the volume of national income also becomes smaller. The problem has no solution which would be entirely satisfactory from a logical point of view. The fact simply has to be accepted that all coefficients (quite apart from their margin of uncertainty), have a "margin of indeterminateness". The width of this margin is given by the maximum possible relative spread of the deflators involved. As a practical measure it would seem reasonable to choose a coefficient on the basis of the average for the whole period under consideration. This can be achieved by expressing both

E

series in terms of constant prices for the average of the entire period for which the calculation is made.[1]

## 6. SEPARATION OF WORLD TRADE IN ITS TWO MAIN COMPONENTS

We have indicated in Chapter IV our preference for world trade to be used as a factor explaining the exports of an individual country rather than world income. One of the principles underlying this choice was that in order to single out the specific factors affecting a country's exports it is desirable to eliminate beforehand the general factors which affect the exports of all countries. This same principle has to be carried one step farther in our practical statistical applications, by eliminating in advance also the factors which affect the exports of a large group of countries. The pattern of world trade in its two main categories—(i) primary products (raw materials and foodstuffs)[2] and (ii) manufactured articles—is rather different, and the fluctuations in any country's exports will depend to a considerable extent on the composition of these exports and the extent, accordingly, to which the country partakes in the different fluctuations shown by the different categories. A separate treatment of the different categories is, therefore, necessary.

---

[1] It is to be noted that the problem is purely one of relative prices, not one of index numbers. It presents itself also where the two variables compared are not aggregates but individual commodities. Thus if someone consumes two lumps of sugar with every cup of coffee, any attempt to express in one coefficient his marginal propensity to consume sugar, given his consumption of coffee, would run into the same difficulty. At a price ratio of 1 : 10 for one lump of sugar to one cup of coffee, the propensity would be ·2; but at a price ratio of 1 : 20, the propensity would be ·1. In order to arrive at a determinate figure it would be necessary to choose, somewhat arbitrarily, *the* value ratio of coffee to sugar, for which the average of a certain period would appear most suitable.

[2] Unfortunately, data for world trade in foodstuffs and raw materials are not available prior to 1929; it would certainly have been preferable to use these groups separately if this had been possible.

## 7. THE TREATMENT OF INVISIBLES

The terms imports and exports have so far been used without precise definition. It is clear that ideally in our system they should be interpreted to refer to all current items in the balance of payments. But for practical purposes varying definitions have to be adopted at various stages of our analysis. Thus, in explaining the exports of a country, we take into consideration only the commodity exports. Too little information is available to explain the "volume" of invisible transactions. Gold exports are not included in exports in accordance with the practice established by the Fund for balance of payments statistics.[1] In the case of countries which do not produce gold, this is obvious: for such countries the export of gold represents a balancing item. For the gold-producing countries, it is logical to treat gold production as the equivalent of commodity exports; for the *production* of gold creates both income at home and results in an increase in the country's foreign assets, while the *export* of gold merely leads to a change in the form of the foreign assets (*e.g.* from gold holdings to dollar or sterling holdings). Since, however, the production of gold is determined by factors quite different from those determining the production of other commodities for export, gold production has not been incorporated in the explanation of the volume of exports for any country.

In the subsequent step, however, where income is explained on the basis of exports, exports can be defined much more broadly. For the countries for which this is important and statistically possible, exports for this purpose are defined as all current items of the balance of payments, including gold production.

[1] *See* International Monetary Fund, *Balance of Payments Manual*, 1948.

## 8. THE COMBINATION OF INSTANTANEOUS AND LAGGED COEFFICIENTS

In a number of instances the correlation could be improved considerably by introducing a lag, *i.e.* by using as explanatory variables the same series (say, $z$) twice, once at year $t$ and once at year $t$-1 (*i.e.* $z_t$ and $z_{t-1}$). Then to express in one number the multiplier or the marginal propensity to import, the coefficients of $z_t$ and $z_{t-1}$ have to be combined into one. In Tinbergen's studies, the sum of the two coefficients was used.[1] It has been pointed out by Verdoorn,[2] however, that the result so obtained is too large. If the regression coefficients of $z_t$ and $z_{t-1}$ are $a_1$ and $a_2$ respectively, the combined coefficient is:

$$\gamma \, (a_1 + a_2) \tag{68·1}$$

where

$$\gamma^2 = \frac{\alpha^2 \Sigma z'_t{}^2 + 2\alpha\beta \Sigma z'_t z'_{t-1} + \beta^2 \Sigma z'_{t-1}{}^2}{\alpha \Sigma z'_t{}^2 + \beta \Sigma z'_{t-1}{}^2} \tag{68·2}$$

in which $\alpha = \dfrac{a_1}{a_1 + a_2}$      $\beta = \dfrac{a_2}{a_1 + a_2}$  (68·3)

and $z'_t$ and $z'_{t-1}$ stand for the deviations of $z_t$ and $z_{t-1}$ from their respective averages.

The adjustment coefficient $\gamma$ based on (68·2) has been used throughout where a combined coefficient on the basis of a lagged influence had to be computed.

---

[1] E.g. *Business Cycles in the United States, 1919–1932*, Geneva 1939.

[2] P. J. Verdoorn, *De Verstarring der Productiekosten* (Increasing Rigidity of Costs of Production), Haarlem, 1943, page 150 *ff.*

# CHAPTER VII

# STATISTICAL RESULTS FOR INDIVIDUAL COUNTRIES

## INTRODUCTION

THIS chapter contains the measurement of three, or in some cases two, basic relationships for individual countries, prefaced by a few lines on the composition and direction of exports. Each relationship is shown in a diagram, usually a time-sequence diagram,[1] which gives separately:

(a) the explained (dependent) variable;

(b) the explanatory (independent) variables multiplied by their regression coefficients;

(c) the weighted sum of the explanatory variables, or the computed value for the explained variable, indicated by an asterisk;

(d) the residual.

The sections on different countries differ greatly in length, depending on the information, statistical or otherwise, available, and any special analyses which seemed necessary or profitable. There is, inevitably, some repetition, in order to make each section readable by itself.

One general point should, however, be made here. In all import and export equations (except a few where the number of observations was very limited) a series on rela-

[1] In some of the diagrams, the units shown differ slightly from those in which the equations are expressed. Thus some index numbers are shown in the diagrams on the base 1927 = 100 or 1929 = 100, while the regression coefficients are based on the average of the period = 100.

tive prices was tried as an explanatory variable. For exports this series represented the export prices of the country under consideration over the corresponding world trade price index (primary articles, manufactures, or total world trade as appropriate). For imports the series represented the import price index, adjusted for tariffs, over the cost of living index. If no price series is shown in the explanation of $x$ or $m$, it should be taken as an indication that no significant coefficient of the proper (negative) sign was found in the correlation.

In the first equation shown (exports of Czechoslovakia) these four elements are as follows:

$(a)$    $x$            : the volume of exports;

$(b)$ $\begin{cases} 1{\cdot}16x_{wm} : \text{the computed influence of changes in} \\ \quad\quad\quad\quad \text{the volume of world trade in manu-} \\ \quad\quad\quad\quad \text{factures on the volume of exports of} \\ \quad\quad\quad\quad \text{Czechoslovakia;} \\ -1{\cdot}08P: \text{the computed influence of changes in} \\ \quad\quad\quad\quad \text{relative prices on the volume of ex-} \\ \quad\quad\quad\quad \text{ports of Czechoslovakia;} \end{cases}$

$(c)$    $x^*$         : the computed volume of exports, $i.e.$
$$1{\cdot}16x_{wm} - 1{\cdot}08P$$

$(d)$    $x - x^*$   : the residual, or unexplained part, of the volume of exports.

In all cases where the import equations show a pronounced shift between the 'twenties and the 'thirties, a separate section is added in order to derive the multiplier for the second period on the basis of the multiplier for one period, the two values for the marginal propensity to import, and the assumption of a constant value for $\delta$.

Of the twenty-five countries analysed, twenty-four are arranged in four groups—Europe, British Dominions, Far East and Latin America—and alphabetically within each group. The United States, for which measurement of the multiplier presents a particular problem, is treated last.

A synoptic table of results will be found in the next chapter.

# CZECHOSLOVAKIA

## I

Czechoslovakia's exports consisted mainly of manufactured products which in 1929 amounted to 72 per cent of the total. They included a great variety of commodities, the most important of which were textiles, metal goods and machinery, glass, ceramics, and leather manufactures. The main markets for these exports were in Europe, with Germany and Austria as the largest customers.

The explanation of fluctuations in the volume of exports was limited to the period from 1924 to 1932 as the index does not exist for later years. The standard explanatory variables, the volume of world trade in manufactures $(x_{wm})$, and an index $P$, representing the relative export prices of Czechoslovakia compared to world trade prices of manufactures, were used with the following results:

$$x = 1 \cdot 16 x_{wm} - 1 \cdot 08 P \qquad R = 0 \cdot 98$$

The price coefficient indicates a mean elasticity of $-1 \cdot 08$.

## II

A satisfactory explanation of fluctuations in real income could be obtained by correlation with $f$ (commodity exports plus income on account of invisibles deflated by the import price index) plus autonomous imports:

$$y = 2 \cdot 55 \, (f + m_A) \qquad R = 0 \cdot 98$$

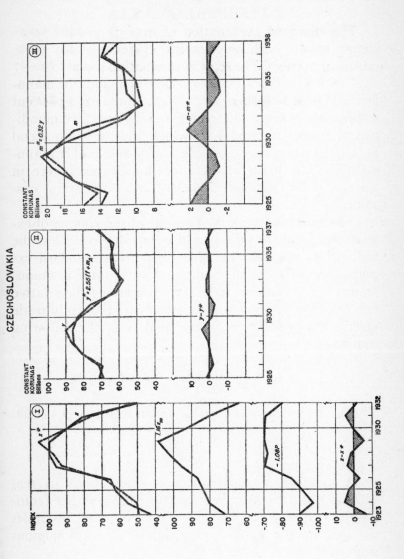

CZECHOSLOVAKIA

## III

The standard explanation of imports yielded satisfactory results, with no statistical evidence of any price substitution effect. The regression equation was as follows:

$$m = 0 \cdot 32 \, y \qquad\qquad R = 0 \cdot 95$$

# DENMARK

## I

Denmark exports mainly foodstuffs, bacon and butter constituting nearly half of total exports in 1937. More than one-half of total Danish exports went to the United Kingdom.

The explanation of the volume of exports of Denmark in a manner similar to that of other countries presents unusual difficulties. The curve of exports, shown in Diagram I, indicates the nature of these difficulties. It is true that two parts of the curve can be attributed to conventional causes: the low in 1924 to 1926, when prices in Denmark were high due to the sudden appreciation of the Danish currency, and the general cyclical pattern in the late 'thirties. But no ready explanation is available for the steady rise from 1929 to 1931 and the continued high level in 1932. It is curious, however, that the food import index in the United Kingdom shows the same pattern, although no explanation can be found for it in terms of the variables which determine the fluctuations in United Kingdom food imports in other years.[1] In Diagram I, the volume of Danish exports is shown as related to the volume of United Kingdom food imports $[m_{f(UK)}]$, the relationship being as follows:

$$x = 2 \cdot 53 m_{f(UK)} \qquad\qquad R = 0 \cdot 85$$

No effect of price substitution could be found.

[1] Hans Neisser and Franco Modigliani, *National Income and International Trade* (Studies of the Institute of World Affairs), (To be published in 1953).

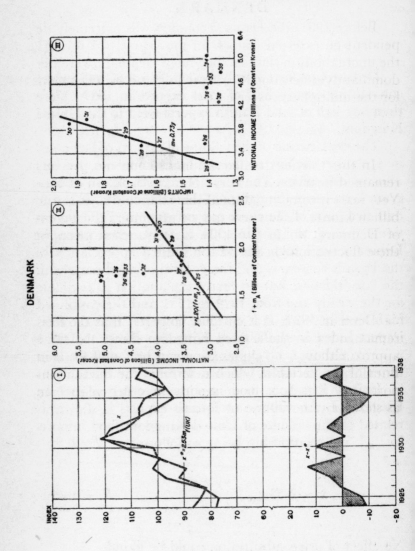

DENMARK

## II

Before 1931, the Danish economy was extremely dependent on external factors. In the years 1925 to 1931, the fluctuations in the real income of Denmark were predominantly determined by those in $f$ and $m_A$. The value for the multiplier was given by:

$$y = 1 \cdot 20 \, (f + m_A) \qquad\qquad R = 0 \cdot 99$$

In the 'thirties the determinant of income, $f + m_A$, remained nearly constant at about $1 \cdot 75$ billion kroner. Yet real income fluctuated between $4 \cdot 27$ and $5 \cdot 05$ billion kroner. A further study of the internal economy of Denmark would probably be required to explain these fluctuations in national income.

## III

Denmark's imports, like her exports in real terms, remained practically constant in the 'thirties at approximately $1 \cdot 4$ billion kroner, while $y$ fluctuated. But during the earlier period, 1923-31, changes in imports were closely associated with those in real income, as shown by the following equation:

$$m = 0 \cdot 73 \, y \qquad\qquad R = 0 \cdot 94$$

# FINLAND

## I

Finnish exports were heavily concentrated on wood and its products which together accounted for 84 per cent of exports in 1937.

The curve of Finnish exports shows a sharp rise after 1933, which should be attributed, at least to a considerable extent, to the building boom in the United Kingdom. In 1937 43 per cent of the exports of Finland were sold to the United Kingdom. Two alternative explanations of the fluctuations in $x$ were attempted. In the explanation shown in Diagram Ib, building activity in the United Kingdom $(B)$ was introduced as a separate variable in addition to the volume of world trade in primary commodities $(x_{wp})$. This explanation yielded the following result:

$$x = 0\cdot26\, x_{wp} + 0\cdot84\, B \qquad\qquad R = 0\cdot95$$

It would seem, however, that in this explanation the variable $B$ has absorbed a considerable part of the normal cyclical fluctuation in exports: the coefficient $0\cdot26$ for $x_{wp}$ would appear to be too low. An alternative explanation was therefore attempted without the variable $B$, but including in addition to $x_{wp}$ both a trend $(t)$ and a trend break between 1931 and 1932 $(T)$. A similar trend break is also used in the explanation of exports of two other northern countries, Norway and Sweden, which were in a position somewhat similar to that of Finland with respect to their export products and their export markets.

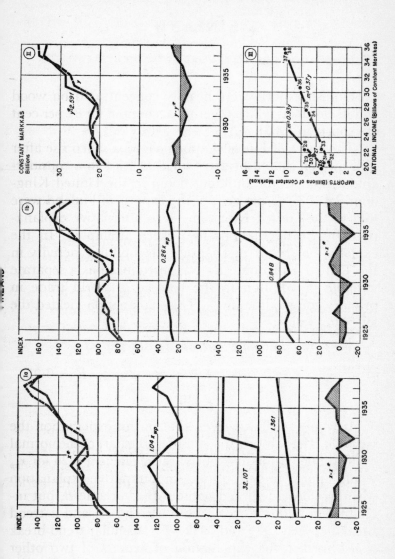

The equation for the alternative explanation is as follows:

$$x = 1 \cdot 04 \, x_{wp} + 1 \cdot 36 \, t + 32 \cdot 10 \, T \qquad R = 0 \cdot 96$$

This equation has been used in the general system.

## II

Correlation of real income with $f$ (all credit items of the current account of the balance of payments deflated by the import price index) yielded the following result:

$$y = 2 \cdot 59 \, f \qquad\qquad R = 0 \cdot 96$$

In this calculation no allowance was made for $m_A$ since the import equation showed a perfect correlation over the period from 1932 to 1938 and the data for the earlier period appeared too uncertain. The value for the multiplier of $2 \cdot 59$ has been assumed to be applicable to the second period as it accounts for most of the fluctuation in $y$ and $f$; the multiplier for the earlier period is computed below.

## III

As shown by Diagram III the relationship between the volume of imports and real national income displays two distinct periods, from 1926 to 1931, and from 1932 to 1938. A separate correlation was made for both periods with the following results:

(a) For 1926–31:
$$m = 0 \cdot 93 \, y \qquad\qquad R = 0 \cdot 84$$
(b) For 1932–38:
$$m = 0 \cdot 37 \, y \qquad\qquad R = 1 \cdot 00$$

It may be doubted whether the marginal propensity to import for the first period was actually as high as the first correlation indicates. In the absence of further information we have, however, accepted the figure found.

## IV

The multiplier for the first period is found as follows:

| | | | |
|---|---|---|---|
| Second period | Multiplier | 2·59 |
| | $(\text{Multiplier})^{-1}$ | 0·39 |
| | $\mu$ | 0·37 |
| First period | $\delta$ | 0·02 |
| | $\mu$ | 0·93 |
| | $(\text{Multiplier})^{-1}$ | 0·95 |
| | Multiplier | 1·05 |

F

# FRANCE

## I

The exports of France in 1929 consisted of about one-third primary articles (13 per cent foodstuffs, 20 per cent raw materials) and two-thirds manufactured products. Separate equations were fitted to explain the fluctuations in the exports of primary products $(x_p)$ and in the exports of manufactured products $(x_m)$. In both correlations the relevant series of world trade, relative export prices and a trend were used with the following results:

$$x_p = 1 \cdot 10\, x_{wp} - 0 \cdot 31\, P_p - 2 \cdot 29\, t \qquad R = 0 \cdot 90$$

$$x_m = 0 \cdot 72\, x_{wm} - 0 \cdot 24\, P_m - 5 \cdot 22\, t \qquad R = 0 \cdot 97$$

The two coefficients for $P$ indicate the mean price elasticities in the two relationships. A negative trend of about 2 per cent for primary products and 5 per cent for manufactured products appears from the formulæ.

## II

An estimation of the multiplier for France poses various difficulties. In the first place the national income data at current prices may be considered to be relatively inaccurate, and the inaccuracies may have increased by deflation. Secondly, the deflated series shows relatively little fluctuation. Thirdly, the multiplicand should incorporate not only $f$ and $m_A$, but also changes in the budget deficit. It is, however, difficult to obtain reliable data for this factor; data on changes in the government debt (domestic or total) give an entirely different picture than

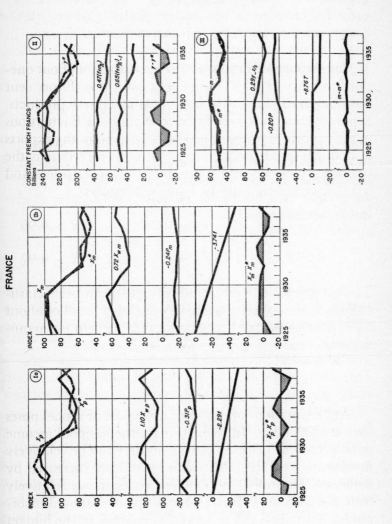

data based on reported revenue and expenditure (including various types of extraordinary expenditure). It proved, finally, that the use of $(f + m_A)$ without adjustment for changes in the budget deficit gave a notably better correlation than the use of figures adjusted by either of the two available series for the budget deficit. Hence we selected, reluctantly, a correlation of the form

$$y = 0\cdot47 \; (f + m_A) + 0\cdot65 \; (f + m_A)_{-1} \qquad R = 0\cdot87$$

with a lag of over half a year. The multiplier is extremely low: $1\cdot12$; and in these circumstances there is no good justification for the lag found, as the primary effect, equivalent to a multiplier of unity, should presumably occur instantaneously.

### III

In view of the doubtful quality of the series for $y$, discussed in the preceding section, it was not likely that a good explanation of imports could be obtained, and the actual result found, although yielding a satisfactory degree of correlation, should be accepted with considerable hesitation. Inspection of the data of $m$ and $y$ seemed to indicate a lag of imports with respect to national income of about two-thirds of a year. Hence a series for $y$ lagged by that period (weighted average of last year's income with a weight of two-thirds and this year's income with a weight of one-third) was used in the correlation. Two other variables were included, the import price index over the cost of living index $(P)$ and a trend break between 1931 and 1932 $(T)$. With these variables the following regression equation was obtained:

$$m = 0\cdot25 \; y_{-\frac{2}{3}} - 0\cdot20 \; P - 8\cdot76 \; T \qquad R = 0\cdot94$$

The mean price elasticity was $-0.40$. The trend break (which is expressed in an arbitrary unit) should be attributed to tariff increases (to the extent that they are not adequately reflected in the $P$ series) and quantitative import restrictions.

# GERMANY

## I

Germany's exports consisted predominantly of industrial commodities. In 1929 manufactures accounted for 78 per cent of exports (rails, structural iron, etc., 15 per cent, chemicals 12 per cent, machinery 11 per cent, electrical equipment 8 per cent, etc.). The remainder of exports consisted mainly of raw materials with coal and coke accounting for 6 per cent of total exports. The explanation of the volume of German exports (excluding reparations in kind) was limited to the period 1923 to 1932 as it was expected that other factors than those which could be statistically accounted for might have had a considerable effect on exports in the later years of the 'thirties. Actually the data for the later 'thirties do not deviate much from values computed on the basis of the correlation found for the earlier period. The correlation is as follows:

$$x = 0.33 \, x_{wm} + 1.11 \, (x_{wm})_{-1} \qquad R = 0.97$$

As in other countries of the continent of Europe, it was necessary to include a lagged term for $x_{wm}$. The average lag as indicated by the coefficients would work out at 0.77 year. The elasticity of demand for German exports with respect to the world trade in manufactured commodities works out at slightly less than the sum of the two coefficients,[1] namely, 1.36.

## II

The derivation of a multiplier for Germany presents

[1] *Cf.* page 70.

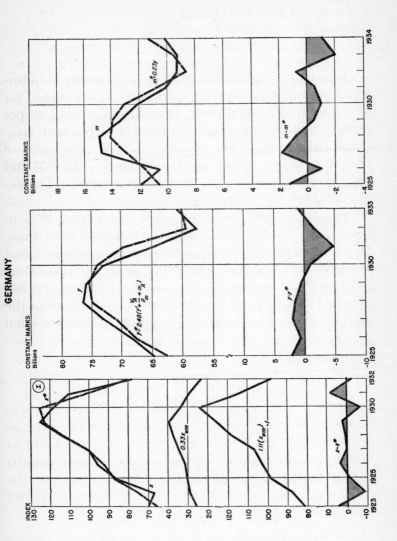

difficulties from various points of view. In the first place Germany is the outstanding country for which it is necessary to take account of the inflow of capital in addition to fluctuations in exports. Secondly, the extreme shift in the German balance of payments after 1929, changing radically the relation of imports to exports, makes the standard treatment of deflation of exports by the import price index inadmissible and requires the alternative treatment indicated in Chapter II. We use, therefore, $f'$ instead of $f$. Thirdly, it is clear that the public works and rearmament programme in the later 'thirties would make for a level of income much higher than could be expected on the basis of the foreign factors; accordingly our correlation has to be limited to the earlier period.

The choice of a proper series for the relevant capital imports $(V_A)$ is particularly difficult. We have tentatively selected for this series available data on gross long-term plus short-term capital imports excluding the movement of existing securities and repayment of loans. The figures obtained on this basis, added to the figures for commodity exports and adjusted for changes in the price level of imports, together with $f'$ and $m_A$, have been used to determine the multiplier for the years 1925 through 1933:[1]

$$y = 2 \cdot 48 \left( f' + \frac{V_A}{P_m} + m_A \right) \qquad R = 0 \cdot 95$$

### III

The import equation for Germany was found to be as follows for the period 1925–34:

$$m = 0 \cdot 23 \, y \qquad R = 0 \cdot 87$$

The correlation coefficient is rather unsatisfactory but no plausible way of improving it seemed indicated.

[1] The diagram has been drawn in terms of the 1929 prices showing an approximate multiplier of $2 \cdot 0$ in those units.

# HUNGARY

## I

In 1937, 57 per cent of Hungary's exports consisted of foodstuffs and another 13 per cent of raw materials. Cereals and meat were most important among the exported foodstuffs. Germany, Austria, and Italy were the three most important markets, accounting together for over 50 per cent of Hungary's exports.

No really satisfactory explanation could be obtained of the fluctuations in exports. The formula finally selected was the following:

$$x = 1 \cdot 59 \, x_{wp} \qquad\qquad R = 0 \cdot 78$$

The correlation coefficient in this explanation is low, far lower than that accepted in the explanation of exports for any other country. Attempts to improve the correlation by including a relative price series or series indicating fluctuations in the volume of agricultural products were not successful.

## II

In establishing a series of the foreign factors for Hungary the inclusion of capital imports is of great importance as both long-term and short-term loans were an important stimulant of domestic activity in the period from 1925 to 1930. On the average for those years they amounted to about one-third of the value of exports. The series $f$, therefore, represents the sum of all current credit items in the balance of payments plus the increase in foreign indebtedness (positive figures only) deflated by

the import price index, the following correlation re-
platting the deviation in time-quadrant: in the order

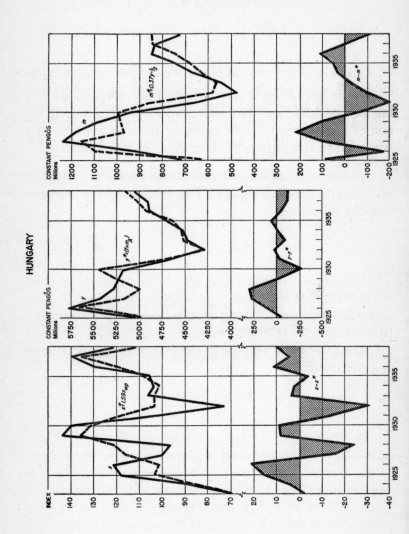

HUNGARY

the import price index. The following correlation, explaining fluctuations in $y$, was found on this basis:

$$y = 1 \cdot 80 \, (f + m_A) \qquad\qquad R = 0 \cdot 93$$

### III

In the import equation it seemed necessary to allow a lag of one-half year between imports and national income. For this purpose a two-year moving average of $y$ was used in this equation. The result was as follows:

$$m = 0 \cdot 37 \, y_{-\frac{1}{2}} \qquad\qquad R = 0 \cdot 85$$

# IRELAND

## I

More than three-fourths of the exports of Ireland in 1937 consisted of foodstuffs (live animals, meat, dairy products, beverages, etc.). More than 90 per cent of the exports were directed to the British market. The following explanation was found for fluctuations in exports:

$$x = 1 \cdot 03 \, x_{wp} - 3 \cdot 07 \, t \qquad\qquad R = 0 \cdot 90$$

Attempts to improve the correlation by including relative prices or an index of crops were not successful.

## II

In the absence of national income data a direct relationship was fitted between $m$ and $f$ (allowing in the latter for invisible credit items in the balance of payments) with the following result:

$$m = 0 \cdot 47 \, f - 0 \cdot 50 \, t \qquad\qquad R = 0 \cdot 93$$

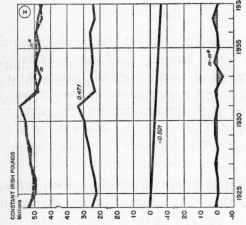

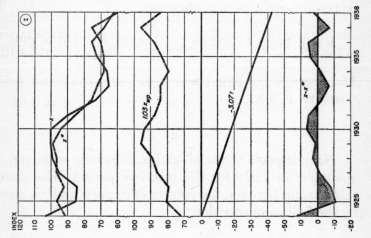

IRELAND

# ITALY

### I

Italy's exports varied over a wide range of commodities including, in 1929, roughly one-fourth foodstuffs, one-fourth raw materials, and one-half manufactured products. Italy's markets were mainly in Europe and in its colonies. In view of the diverse nature of exports, the volume of world trade as a whole $(x_w)$ was selected as the main explanatory variable. Allowance was made for a lag by including $(x_w)_{-1}$, and a series indicating the ratio of Italian export prices to prices of world trade in general $(P)$ was also included. On account of the deleterious effect on exports of the war against Ethiopia and sanctions, the years 1934 to 1936 were omitted. The following regression equation was obtained:

$$x = 0.44\, x_w + 0.37\, (x_w)_{-1} - 0.53\, P \qquad R = 0.95$$

The average lag found was $0.46$ year; the mean price elasticity $-0.53$.

### II

No adequate series of national income estimates is available for Italy for the interwar period. The direct relationship between the volume of imports and $f$ is given by the following equation:

$$m = 1.17 f \qquad\qquad R = 0.84$$

In Diagram II, $m$ and $f$ are both shown as index numbers, with the base year 1927 = 100. In 1927 (and

ITALY

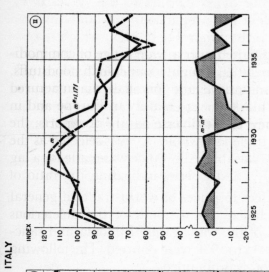

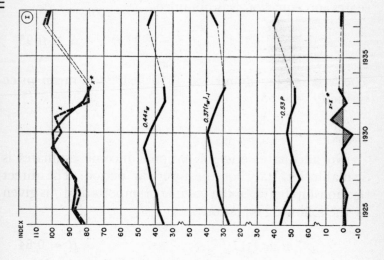

throughout the period) imports were considerably larger than exports. If it may be assumed, however, that invisible receipts, which were approximately equal to the import surplus, fluctuated parallel to the values of exports, the coefficient 1·17 would constitute an estimate of $\rho$. The figure is rather improbably high, which may be attributable to the quality of the statistics or the inadequacy of the correlation. In the absence of further information, and since coefficients for other countries may have downward biases due to similar causes, it seems best to retain the figure as it follows from the correlation.

## NETHERLANDS

### I

The exports of the Netherlands are widely distributed over the main groups of the Brussels Classification, as is indicated by the following percentages applicable to 1938 statistics:

|  | Per cent of Total Exports |
|---|---|
| Foodstuffs | 33 |
| Raw Materials | 24 |
| Manufactured Goods | 43 |
|  | 100 |

Although manufactures account for less than one-half of total exports, the index of the world trade in manufactures was selected as the main explanatory variable on the assumption that the foodstuffs exported by the Netherlands were subjected to a market demand more similar to that of manufactured goods than to that of primary articles. Two subsidiary explanatory variables were included in the correlation, *viz.* the relative price of Netherlands exports to prices of manufactures in world trade in general $(P)$ and a trend $(t)$. The result was as follows:

$$x = 0.92\ x_{wm} - 0.92\ P + 0.57\ t \qquad R = 0.94$$

The price coefficient indicates a mean price elasticity of $-0.92$.

### II

Diagram II for the Netherlands compares the fluctuations in real income and the foreign factors, the latter measured in the usual way, and allowance being made for $m_A$. The relationship between the two variables is by no means pronounced. The points from 1925 to 1929 would appear to lie on a line indicating a multiplier of about 2, but the shift of the curve to the right between 1929 and 1930 would seem difficult to explain. It is curious, also, that from 1933 to 1937 the foreign factors increased more than real national income (726 million of constant guilders for the former as against 360 million for the latter). This would indicate a multiplier of less than unity, which seems impossible.

There may be two reasons why the multiplier for the Netherlands cannot be found by the same method as for most other countries. In the first place the actual fluctuations in real income were extremely small, with the 1934 low only 10 per cent below the 1929 peak level. Compared with such small fluctuations, the errors in the figures for money national income and the cost of living index, and hence in the real income series itself, would be large proportionally. The lack of correlation between $y$ and the foreign factors may, therefore, be due to errors in the income series. Secondly, the fluctuations in the foreign factors themselves consist of a number of elements, each of which fluctuates very largely while the resulting net figure for $f$ does not fluctuate very much. The very sharp fall in export value and invisible receipts from 1929–30 to 1933 or 1934 was offset by an almost equally large fall, proportionally, in the import price index. Here, again, there is the possibility of minor errors of measurement appearing as large compared with the small net change of $f$; and there is the further possibility that two large offsetting changes do not have exactly offsetting effects. Thus the multiplier applicable to a fall in income from foreign investment may have been different from the multiplier applicable to an increase in the real income of labour due to lower import prices. In that

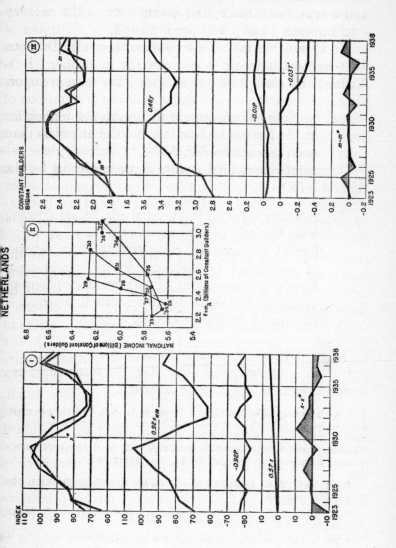

case, if the two "primary" effects are equal and of opposite sign, the secondary effects will be different in size,
and a real, not a statistical, discrepancy in the relationship between $f$ and $y$ will present itself.

In view of the lack of correlation shown by Diagram
II it seemed desirable to estimate the multiplier for the
Netherlands along other lines. Two other ways are open:

(a) Various calculations of the multiplier were made
in the Netherlands in the 'thirties along the lines
first proposed by Mr. Kahn.[1] Generally these calculations yielded results in the order of 1·40 to
1·75.[2]

(b) Another estimate may be made by computing,
with the help of Tinbergen's system of equations
for the Netherlands' economy, the total amount
of additional employment which would result
from a given amount of additional employment
on public works, or on investment in general. In
this way a multiplier of 1·56 is found.[3]

The various figures are reasonably close, and none
can claim complete perfection. On the basis of all evidence a figure of 1·6 may be accepted.[4]

---

[1] R. F. Kahn, "The Relation of Home Investment to Unemployment",
*Economic Journal*, 41 (1931), pages 173–198. This method, it may be recalled, consisted in estimating in what proportions amounts spent on public works would be
distributed over wages, profits and imports; estimating the marginal propensity to
consume of wage-earners and of capitalists, and making some allowance for price
rises.

[2] J. J. Polak, *Public Works as a Form of Business Cycle Policy* (in Dutch), The
Hague, 1938, page 18.

[3] J. J. Polak, "The International Propagation of Business Cycles", *Review of
Economic Studies*, Vol. VI, February 1939.

[4] The lack of determinacy of the multiplier on account of the choice of the
base year for price indices, to which reference was made in Chapter VI, is particularly acute in this case, where the 1924–1938 average of the cost of living index
(base 1929 = 100) is 19 per cent higher than the average of the import price index
on the same base.

## III

With respect to the explanation of fluctuations in imports we can fall back on a recent study by Tinbergen.[1] In it, a variety of possible explanations is given for raw materials and finished goods separately; using the combined data a correlation for the volume of total imports has been recomputed as follows:

$$m = 0.48\,y - 0.01\,P - 0.03\,T' \qquad R = 0.97$$

The mean price elasticity is $-0.30$. The series $T'$ is used as an indicator (expressed in arbitrary units) of the effect of quantitative restrictions. Its value for any year $t$ was obtained by adding the 1929 value of imports of all commodities which were subject to quantitative restrictions in the year $t$. The relative importance of $T'$ was determined by the multiple correlation calculation.

[1] J. Tinbergen, "De schommelingen van de invoer, 1923–1938" (Fluctuations in Imports, 1923–1938), *Statistische en Econometrische Onderzoekingen*, 1948, No. 2, pages 1–9.

# NORWAY

## I

Norway's exports consisted for over 60 per cent of industrial raw materials (timber, pulp, metals and minerals); 20 per cent foodstuffs (mainly fish and fishery products); and the remainder manufactured products. Three-fourths of her exports were directed to other European countries of which the United Kingdom (25 per cent) and Germany (13 per cent) were the most important.

In explaining fluctuations in the volume of Norway's exports it appeared necessary, as in the case of Finland and Sweden, to include a trend break series $(T)$ which stood for an increase of the level of imports, at a constant rate of world trade in primary products, in the years from 1932 on as compared with the previous years. As indicated by the following equation:

$$x = 1 \cdot 05 \ x_{wp} + 30 \cdot 2 \ T \qquad\qquad R = 0 \cdot 94$$

the trend break accounted for a rise in the volume of exports by as much as 30 per cent of the average interwar volume of exports.

Various factors contributed to the favourable development of Norway's exports in the 'thirties. Two of these may be mentioned:

(1) the increasing importance of various "new" commodities such as nitrate of lime, nickel, zinc, and silver fox furs. These commodities which were

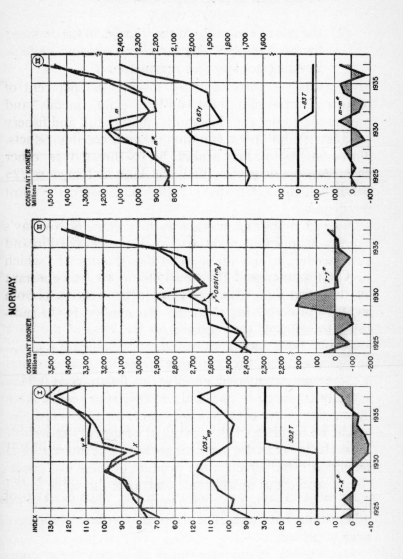

NORWAY

insignificant in the exports in 1929 accounted for 13 per cent of total exports in 1938.[1]

(2) the relative increase in the 'thirties in the demand for both lumber and metals on account of high building activity and rearmament.

## II and III

The two following equations explaining fluctuations in real national income and in the volume of imports are unsatisfactory despite a relatively high degree of correlation:

$$y = 0{\cdot}69 \ (f + m_A) \qquad\qquad R = 0{\cdot}95$$
$$m = 0{\cdot}67 \, y - 83 \ T \qquad\qquad R = 0{\cdot}97$$

On the one hand the multiplier is far below unity; on the other hand the marginal propensity to import seems improbably high at $0{\cdot}67$. No solution seems indicated to improve these results on the basis of the data available. Both anomalies would be explained if it could be assumed that the available series for real national income underestimated greatly the fluctuations which actually occurred in national income. If in reality these fluctuations were considerably larger, the true multiplier would be higher and the marginal propensity to import would be lower in the same proportion. The international reflection ratio, which is the product of these two coefficients, would not be affected; and since the value found for it $(0{\cdot}46)$ does not compare unreasonably with that for other somewhat similar countries, the two equations have been accepted.

[1] Erling Petersen, *Memorandum on the Repercussions of Modern Commercial Policies on the Economic Conditions in Norway* (Bergen General Study Conference on Economic Policies in Relation to World Peace, 1939).

# SWEDEN

## I

The exports of Sweden were distributed about equally over raw materials and manufactured products. Among the raw materials wood pulp and iron ore were the most important; among the manufactured products, high-quality machinery and specialized products took a large place. Three-fourths of Sweden's exports in 1937 went to other European countries with the United Kingdom and Germany together accounting for 40 per cent of the total.

In the explanation of the volume of Swedish exports a trend break series ($T$) was included as in the case of Finland and Norway, in addition to the index of total world trade ($x_w$):

$$x = 1 \cdot 61 \, x_w + 31 \cdot 80 \, T \qquad R = 0 \cdot 98$$

The year 1928 was excluded from the calculation on account of the general strike in that year. The high coefficient obtained for $T$ would indicate that Swedish exports in the years from 1933 on were about 32 per cent higher, at constant levels of world trade, than in earlier years. The explanation for this sharp upward trend break should probably be sought in the building boom in the United Kingdom and rearmament.

## II

The explanation of fluctuations in real income was as follows:

$$y = 2 \cdot 53 \, (f + m_A) \qquad R = 0 \cdot 96$$

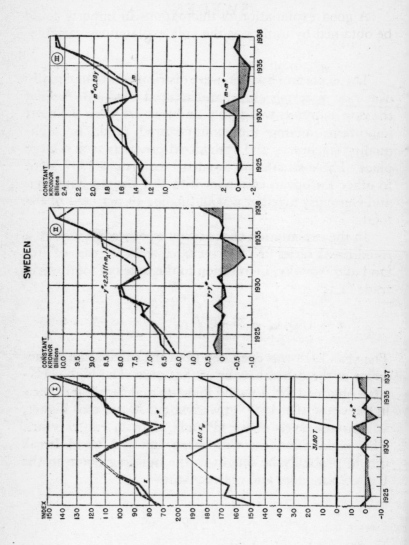

## III

A good explanation of fluctuations in imports could be obtained by using $y$ as the only explanatory variable:

$$m = 0 \cdot 28\, y \qquad\qquad R = 0 \cdot 97$$

# SWITZERLAND

## I

In 1929, 80 per cent of Switzerland's exports consisted of manufactured articles. An explanation of fluctuations in exports was found by using the three following variables: the index of world trade in manufactured goods $(x_{wm})$, the relative export prices of manufactures of Switzerland compared to the prices of other countries $(P)$, and a trend $(t)$:

$$x = 1 \cdot 10\, x_{wm} - 0 \cdot 16\, P - 2 \cdot 43\, t \qquad R = 0 \cdot 99$$

The mean elasticity found was $- 0 \cdot 16$. The trend assumed a very high negative slope (nearly $2\frac{1}{2}$ per cent $p.\,a.$ of the average volume of exports).

## II

It was not possible to include in the series $f$ used in the explanation of fluctuations in $y$ any information on fluctuations on invisible income (tourist receipts, interest receipts, etc.) which constitute an important element in the balance of payments of Switzerland. In the following equation therefore $f$ stands for the value of exports deflated by the import price index only. The years 1924 to 1933 yielded a high correlation and a plausible value for the multiplier if a trend was included.

$$y = 1 \cdot 55\, (f + m_A) + 0 \cdot 25\, t \qquad R = 0 \cdot 99$$

The equation contains a high positive trend which may represent an increasing relative importance of invisibles to commodity exports; it may also at least in part

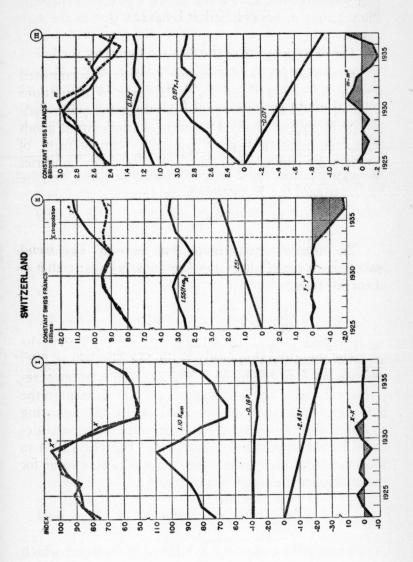

be due to some systematic error in the $y$ series, in which case the large negative trend in the equation explaining fluctuations in imports might be partly due to the same cause.

The extrapolation of the formula found for the following years gave a very unsatisfactory result, as the diagram shows, with $(f + m_A)$ and the trend rising while $y$ remained about constant; and no satisfactory explanation of fluctuations in $y$ for the period as a whole could be obtained. This may be due to the weaknesses in the national income series or in the $f$ series, or to the difficulties in deflation similar to those encountered, for instance, in the case of the Netherlands.

## III

The import equation yielded an only moderately satisfactory result after allowing for a lag and a sharply negative trend:

$$m = 0.12\,y + 0.27\,y_{-1} - 0.81\,t \qquad R = 0.86$$

The marginal propensity to import obtained by combining the coefficients for $y$ and $y_{-1}$ works out at 0.36.[1]

---

[1] Cf. page 70.

# UNITED KINGDOM

## I

In 1937, United Kingdom exports consisted for 80 per cent of manufactured products (textiles 29 per cent, machinery 12 per cent, iron and steel 8 per cent). Although exports of primary products constituted only a relatively small proportion of total exports (foodstuffs 8 per cent, raw materials 12 per cent, of which 8 per cent coke and coal) their absolute magnitude was sufficient to justify a separate explanation. A weighted average of the indices of the volume of exports of foodstuffs and raw materials was therefore computed $(x_p)$ and an explanation of it was sought by reference to fluctuations in the volume of world trade in primary products $(x_{wp})$ and relative prices:

$$x_p = 0.33\, x_{wp} - 0.92\, P_p \qquad\qquad R = 0.90$$

A similar explanation of the exports of manufactured products, in which a trend was included, yielded the following result:

$$x_m = 0.75\, x_{wm} - 1.49\, t \qquad\qquad R = 0.89$$

## II

The importance of commodity exports and income on account of invisibles was considerably less in the British economy in the 'thirties than in the 'twenties. On the average foreign exchange revenue on current account was 31 per cent of national income in the 'twenties as against 26 per cent in the 'thirties. In explaining fluctuations in national income account had to be taken of the

UNITED KINGDOM-I

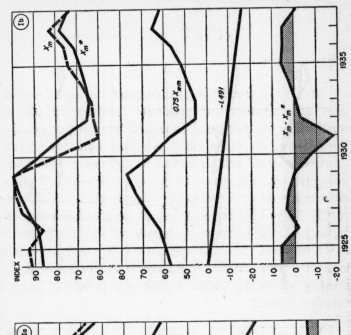

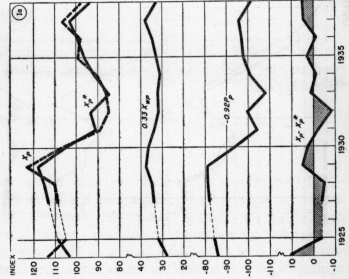

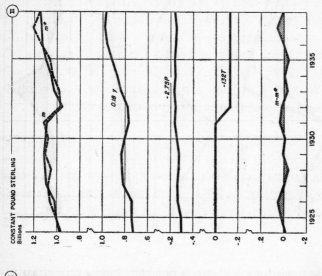

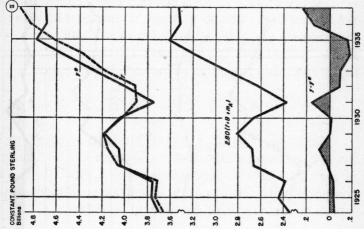

building boom of the 'thirties which, although partly due to such endogenous factors as the fall in the cost of living, must be attributed to a considerable extent to exogenous factors such as the government's interest policy.[1] For this reason a series $B$ was added to $f$ and $m_A$. This series was obtained by deflating a series indicating fluctuations in the value of houses built in each year from 1924 to 1938 by the cost of living index. By using $(f + B + m_A)$ as the multiplicand, the following explanation was obtained for fluctuations in $y$:

$$y = 2 \cdot 80 \ (f + B + m_A) \qquad\qquad R = 0 \cdot 95$$

To the extent that fluctuations in $B$ were in part endogenous, the value of $2 \cdot 80$ found for the multiplier should be considered as somewhat of an underestimate.

### III

A satisfactory, although not very good, explanation of the fluctuations in imports could be obtained by using as explanatory variables $y$, an index of relative prices $(P)$, and a "trend break" $(T)$ between 1931 and 1932, reflecting presumably the effect of increased protection:

$$m = 0 \cdot 18 \ y - 2 \cdot 75 \ P - 132 \ T \qquad R = 0 \cdot 91$$

The coefficient for $T$ would indicate a reduction in imports, at constant levels of real income, of £132 million of average 1924–38 purchasing power in the 'thirties as compared with the 'twenties. The price coefficient corresponds to a mean price elasticity of $- 0 \cdot 24$.

---

[1] For an explanation of the fluctuations in building in the United Kingdom during the interwar period and the relative importance of the various factors contributing to the building boom, *see* J. Tinbergen, *Statistical Testing of Business Cycle Theories*, Vol. I, *A Method and its Application to Investment Activity* (League of Nations, Geneva, 1939), pages 95 *ff*.

# YUGOSLAVIA

## I

Yugoslavia's exports were mainly primary products, with foodstuffs and raw materials each amounting to nearly 50 per cent of the total. The principal individual export commodities were cereals, meats, lumber and ores. The main markets for Yugoslavia's exports before the war were in central Europe. In explaining fluctuations in the volume of exports, two additional variables were used in addition to $x_{wp}$, namely $h$, an index of the crops of corn and wheat, and $T$, a trend starting from 1932. The result was as follows:

$$x = 0 \cdot 91 \, x_{wp} + 0 \cdot 55 \, h - 39 \cdot 64 \, T \qquad R = 0 \cdot 92$$

## II

No continuous national income series for Yugoslavia is available. Data on income from invisibles are also scanty and such income was in any case small compared with export income. Accordingly the $f$ series used in the explanation of $m$ does not make allowance for income on account of invisibles. A small lag between $m$ and $f$ appeared indicated. On this basis the import equation worked out as follows:

$$m = 0 \cdot 84 \, f + 0 \cdot 17 \, f_{-1} - 0 \cdot 14 \, t \qquad R = 0 \cdot 96$$

On the basis of the coefficients for the first two terms on the right-hand side of this equation the international reflection ratio would work out at $0 \cdot 98$.

YUGOSLAVIA

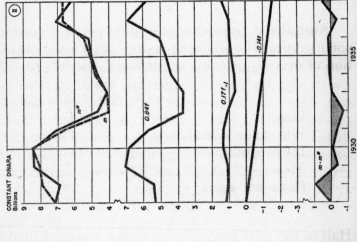

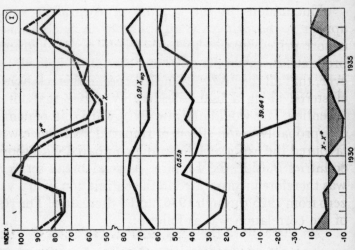

# AUSTRALIA

## I

Australia is predominantly an exporter of primary commodities. The following figures indicate the distribution of over 80 per cent of Australia's exports in 1937:

|  | Per cent of Total Exports |
|---|---|
| Wool | 47 |
| Wheat and Wheat flour | 17 |
| Dairy products | 7 |
| Meats | 7 |
| Hides and skins | 6 |
| Total | 84 |

Half of the total exports went to the United Kingdom.

Fluctuations in the volume of Australia's exports appear to be primarily attributable to fluctuations in export prices relative to world trade prices of primary products. A scatter diagram (not shown) indicated, however, that all the points in the 'thirties in this relationship clustered along a line considerably above that for the 'twenties. This would indicate an upward shift of demand due probably to the effects of Imperial Preference which favoured the exports of Australia compared with those of countries outside the Empire. A trend break series $(T)$ was therefore incorporated in the correlation with a value zero from 1925 through 1930, and 1 thereafter. The result of the correlation was as follows:

$$x = -0.48\,P + 20\,T \qquad\qquad R = 0.99$$

As indicated by the first coefficient the mean price elasticity was $-0.48$.

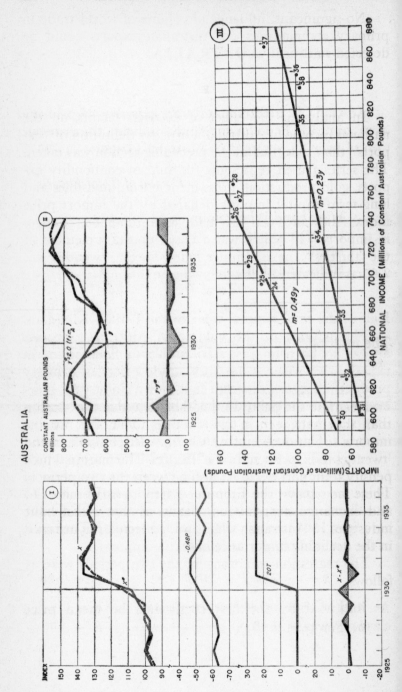

No significant influence of volume of world trade in primary commodities on Australian exports could be detected statistically.

## II

In analysing the effect of external factors on the national income of Australia a broader definition of "exports" than that used in the preceding section was taken. The series $f$ used represents the sum of commodity exports, gold production, gross income from invisibles and long-term capital imports deflated by the import price index. Allowance was also made for autonomous changes in imports $(m_A)$ which was a very important element in the 'thirties. The multiplier found for the 'twenties was 2·00 as indicated by the following equation:

$$y = 2{\cdot}00 \; (f + m_A) \qquad\qquad R = 0{\cdot}90$$

The multiplier for the 'thirties is derived in Section IV.

## III

Australia's imports were notably lower in the 'thirties than they had been in the 'twenties. Thus the ratio of imports to national income fell from 18 per cent in the 'twenties to 11 per cent in the 'thirties. The marginal propensity to import declined also between the two periods. These facts may have been due partly to tariff increases and exchange depreciation, partly to the rise of light industries in Australia, which was reflected for instance in the declining importance of textile imports.

The regression equations for the two periods were as follows:

(a) For 1924 to 1930    $m = 0.49\,y$    $R = 0{\cdot}97$
(b) For 1931 to 1938    $m = 0{\cdot}23\,y$    $R = 0{\cdot}96$

## IV

The multiplier for the 'thirties works out at 4·16, assuming the value for $\delta$ of 0·01 which was found for the 'twenties to be valid also in the 'thirties, and taking into account the greatly reduced value of the marginal propensity to import:

| | | |
|---|---|---|
| 'Twenties | Multiplier | 2·00 |
| | (Multiplier)$^{-1}$ | 0·50 |
| | $\mu$ | 0·49 |
| | $\delta$ | 0·01 |
| 'Thirties | $\mu$ | 0·23 |
| | (Multiplier)$^{-1}$ | 0·24 |
| | Multiplier | 4·16 |

On the basis of the values found for the multiplier and the marginal propensity to import the reflection ratio would work out as nearly unity throughout the period (0·98 and 0·96, respectively).

# CANADA

## I

Canadian exports consisted of a great variety of commodities, mainly primary commodities, which in 1929 accounted for 61 per cent of the total (foodstuffs 38 per cent, raw materials 23 per cent). Among the most important individual commodities were, in 1937, wheat and wheat flour (13 per cent), paper (12 per cent), gold (10 per cent), timber (6 per cent), copper (4 per cent). In 1937, 42 per cent of total exports went to the United States and 30 per cent to the United Kingdom.

In explaining the volume of Canadian exports, gold exports, which are of a special character, have been left out of account. The volume of all other Canadian exports, computed by dividing the value figures by the wholesale export price index, was correlated with the volume of world trade in primary products $(x_{wp})$ and the relative price of Canadian exports over world prices of primary products $(P)$, with the following result:

$$x = 1 \cdot 01 \, x_{wp} - 1 \cdot 56 \, P \qquad\qquad R = 0 \cdot 82$$

It would appear from Diagram I that fluctuations in Canadian exports lead fluctuations in world trade in primary products; no ready explanation for such a lead appears, however, to be available and the lead shown may, in fact, be accidental rather than systematic.

## II

In analysing the effect of exports on national income, a broader definition of "exports" may be used than in the

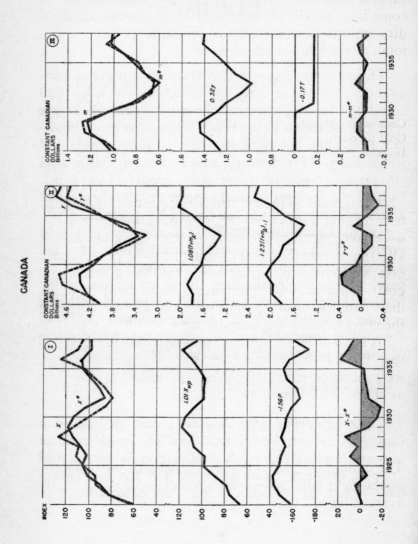

preceding section, including in addition to commodity exports, the value of gold production and invisible income from tourists, interest and other sources. Commodity exports accounted for a declining portion of this total, as the following figures show:

| | *Millions of Canadian Dollars* | | | *Per cent of Total* | | |
|---|---|---|---|---|---|---|
| | *1926* | *1930* | *1939* | *1926* | *1930* | *1939* |
| Commodity exports | 1272 | 880 | 906 | 76 | 68 | 62 |
| Gold production | 30 | 39 | 184 | 2 | 3 | 13 |
| Invisible receipts | 363 | 378 | 367 | 22 | 29 | 25 |
| Total | 1665 | 1297 | 1457 | 100 | 100 | 100 |

In addition to the current account items, gross long-term capital imports in the form of new foreign issues were taken into consideration among the foreign factors affecting national income; in the interwar period, however, in contrast to earlier years, this factor was not of great importance in determining fluctuations in Canadian national income. Allowance was further made for the effect of autonomous imports $(m_A)$.

A lag was found to exist between $y$ and the explanatory factors as indicated; for this reason these factors were incorporated in the correlation both as of year $t$ and as of year $t-1$. The result was as follows:

$$y = 1 \cdot 08 \ (f + m_A) + 1 \cdot 21 \ (f + m_A)_{-1} \quad R = 0 \cdot 91$$

The multiplier based on the coefficients for the two terms on the right-hand side of the equation would be $2 \cdot 13$; the average lag $\cdot 52$ year.

### III

In the explanation of the volume of imports it appeared desirable to incorporate, in addition to real national income, a series reflecting a "trend break" between 1930 and 1931, to take account of the effect of tariff changes in 1930.

$$m = 0\cdot32\,y - 0\cdot17\,T \qquad\qquad R = 0\cdot98$$

where the series $T$ is expressed in billions of Canadian dollars at average 1926–38 purchasing power, indicating a fall in the level of imports of $170 million between the years up to 1930 and those thereafter at constant levels of real income.

# NEW ZEALAND

## I

In 1937 dairy products, wool, and meat together accounted for 90 per cent of the total exports of New Zealand. In that same year 76 per cent of total exports were directed towards the United Kingdom.

A satisfactory explanation for the fluctuation of exports could be found by using the index of world trade in primary products and a trend break occurring between the years 1931 and 1932:

$$x = 0.46\, x_{wp} + 30.5\, T \qquad\qquad R = 0.98$$

The trend coefficient of 30·5 would indicate that New Zealand exports were nearly one-third of their average amount higher after 1931 than before at constant levels of world trade in primary products. The favourable influences of Imperial Preference on New Zealand exports as well as purchase agreements between the United Kingdom and New Zealand probably account for this large upward shift of demand.

## II AND III

Sections II and III are shown for New Zealand in a form somewhat different from that applied for other countries. Scatter Diagrams II and III show $y$ along the vertical axis in both cases, with $f$ along the horizontal axis in II and $m$ in III. It is to be borne in mind that $y$ is the dependent variable in Diagram II and the independent variable in Diagram III. The three series, $y, f$, and $m$, are shown in constant New Zealand pounds. The series $f$ represents the sum of commodity exports, gold production and invisible income, deflated by the import price index.

The two diagrams show a number of interesting features. First, there is a clear break in the two relationships, between 1931 and 1933. At the same value for exports $(f)$, $y$ is much higher in the 'thirties than it was in the 'twenties; similarly, for the same amount of income, imports are much lower in the 'thirties than in the 'twenties. Secondly, the shift in the two relationships between 1931 and 1933, if measured along the income-axis, is practically the same, about £$NZ$35 million at constant prices.[1] Thirdly, the slopes of the relationship change notably between the 'twenties and the 'thirties. As shown in the diagrams, both curves become steeper. In other words the multiplier becomes larger and the marginal propensity to import becomes smaller. A fourth remarkable feature is that three of the four segments show a high degree of correlation. The correlation is poor only for the import equation in the 'twenties, when the data appear to point to a considerable lag between income and imports.

Correlation of the four relationships yielded the following results:

|  |  | $R$ |
|---|---|---|
| *1926–31* | | |
| $y$ | $= 1·06 f$ | 0·95 |
| $m$ | $= 0·51 y$ | 0·65 |

|  |  |  |
|---|---|---|
| *1933–37* | | |
| $y$ | $= 2·64 f$ | 1·00 |
| $m$ | $= 0·47 y$ | 0·95 |

[1] All variables in the diagrams are plotted at 1929 prices. The correlations are made on the basis of average of period (1926–37) prices.

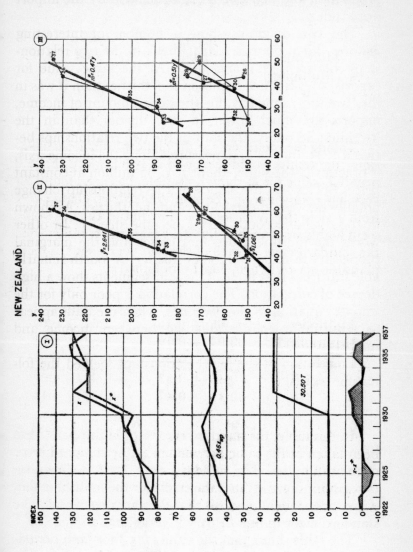

NEW ZEALAND

Taking the four coefficients as found by correlation, we could derive the following values for $\delta$:

|  | *1933–37* | *1926–31* |
|---|---|---|
| Multiplier | 1·06 | 2·64 |
| (Multiplier)$^{-1}$ | 0·94 | 0·38 |
| $\mu$ | 0·51 | 0·47 |
| $\delta$ | 0·43 | − 0·09 |

Taking the coefficients as they follow from the calculations, the results would seem odd in two respects. First, a negative value for $\delta$, though possible, has been found for very few countries only. Secondly, the sharp change in $\delta$ from 0·43 in the 'twenties to − 0·09 in the 'thirties would seem highly improbable. But if we take into consideration the standard error of each of the four coefficients, a more plausible set of figures can be obtained:

|  | *1926–31* | *1933–37* |
|---|---|---|
| Multiplier | 1·06 ± 0·16 | 2·64 ± 0·09 |
| (Multiplier)$^{-1}$ | 0·94 ± 0·14 | 0·38 ± 0·01 |
| $\mu$ | 0·51 ± 0·30 | 0·47 ± 0·07 |
| $\delta$ (i) | 0·43 ± 0·33 | − 0·09 ± 0·07 |
| $\delta$ (ii) | 0·43 ± 0·47 | − 0·09 ± 0·10 |

In this table, the standard error for (Multiplier)$^{-1}$ has been taken as the same percentage as the standard error of the multiplier. The standard error for $\delta$ is shown on two assumptions: (i) that the errors for the multiplier and $\mu$ are independent, and (ii) that they are dependent. The standard error in line (ii) is $\sqrt{2}$ times that on line (i).

The table shows that the values for $\delta$ for both periods are about one standard error different from zero. The difference between the two $\delta$'s (0·52) is about $1\frac{1}{2}$ times its standard error on assumption (i) and slightly over once its standard error on assumption (ii). In the light of all evidence, therefore, it would not seem unreasonable to assume that δ was the same in the two periods, and that in both periods its value was 0 (*i.e.* practically the same as the value found for Australia). This requires adjustments for the μ's and the multipliers, which are inevitably rather arbitrary. It would not seem plausible, *a priori*, that μ in the 'twenties should have been higher than, say, 0·65; the greater part of the adjustment would, therefore, have to be made by changing the multiplier in that period. With respect to the 'thirties a small downward adjustment in the figure for μ and a slight reduction for the multiplier would seem indicated. The revised figures which are rounded for both periods would then work out as follows:

|                    | *1926–31* | *1933–37* |
|--------------------|-----------|-----------|
| Multiplier         | 1·54      | 2·50      |
| (Multiplier)$^{-1}$ | 0·65      | 0·40      |
| μ                  | 0·65      | 0·40      |
| δ                  | 0·00      | 0·00      |

I

## UNION OF SOUTH AFRICA

### I

The main export product of the Union of South Africa is gold. Our explanation of the fluctuation in exports, is however, limited to commodity exports, of which wool was most important, accounting for approximately 30 per cent in 1937.

A reasonably satisfactory explanation of fluctuations in the volume of commodity exports of South Africa could be obtained by including as explanatory variables the volume of world trade in primary products $(x_{wp})$ and the relative prices of South African exports compared with world trade prices of primary products $(P)$:

$$x = 0 \cdot 96\, x_{wp} - 1 \cdot 46\, P \qquad\qquad R = 0 \cdot 88$$

The coefficient for $P$ indicates a mean price elasticity of $-1 \cdot 46$.

### II

In the explanation of the fluctuations of real national income gold production was included as well as income on account of invisibles. In the course of the interwar period the significance of gold, among the credit items on current account, increased greatly, from about 50 per cent in the 'twenties to nearly 75 per cent in 1938.

Diagram II shows a scatter diagram of real income $(y)$ plotted against the foreign factors $(f + m_A)$. The diagram would seem to indicate a horizontal shift in the relationship between 1931 and 1932 by about £SA30 million and a slight increase in the slope.

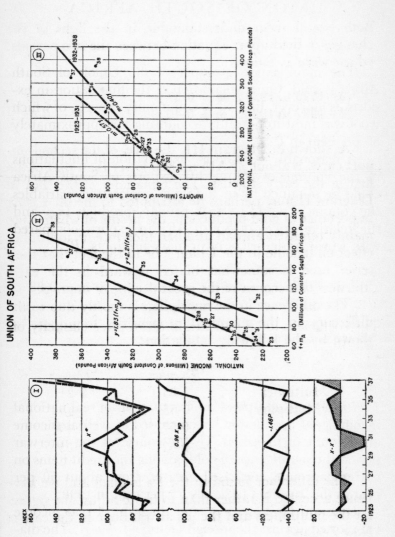

(a) 1923 to 1931:   $y = 1 \cdot 83 \left( f + m_A \right)$    $R = 0 \cdot 91$
(b) 1932 to 1938:   $y = 2 \cdot 21 \left( f + m_A \right)$    $R = 0 \cdot 96$

Both would seem understandable in the light of the changes in the import equation between the two periods, which were as follows:

(a) 1923 to 1931:   $m = 0 \cdot 57 \, y$    $R = 0 \cdot 93$
(b) 1932 to 1938:   $m = 0 \cdot 40 \, y$    $R = 0 \cdot 95$

As shown in Diagram III, the level of the second import curve is about £SA15 million lower than that of the first in the early 'thirties. The remainder of the shift in Diagram II may perhaps be attributed to the increasing importance of gold production, the profits of which were mainly remitted abroad and had therefore no multiplier effect on income in the Union;[1] or to the fact that the $f$ series used is somewhat biased upward in the early 'thirties[2] on account of the great decline of imports.

The difference in the multipliers is mostly due to the difference in the marginal propensities to import, as shown by the following tabulation:

|  | 'Twenties | 'Thirties |
|---|---|---|
| Multiplier | 1·83 | 2·21 |
| (Multiplier)$^{-1}$ | 0·55 | 0·45 |
| μ | 0·57 | 0·40 |
| δ | − 0·02 | 0·05 |

The difference found in the δ's is small and we have hence accepted it rather than to try to adjust the figures for the multipliers and the μ's as was done in the case of New Zealand.

[1] *See* section on Indonesia below.

[2] *See* Chapter II.

# CHINA

## I

The exports of China are mainly primary products. In 1929 foodstuffs accounted for 38 per cent of total exports and raw materials for 47 per cent. The principal export commodities were, in order of importance, beans and beancakes, raw silk, tea and bristles; the main markets, Japan, the United States and the countries of South East Asia.

Fluctuations in the volume of Chinese exports could be explained satisfactorily by the index of world trade in primary products $(x_{wp})$, the appropriate relative price index $(P)$ and a trend $(t)$:

$$x = 1{\cdot}64\,x_{wp} - 0{\cdot}48\,P - 7{\cdot}20\,t \qquad R = 0{\cdot}96$$

The equation indicates a price elasticity of $-0{\cdot}48$. The downward trend may have been due to a decline in foreign demand for typical export products of China such as raw silk, and to the substitution, without noticeable price differential, of the products of other countries for similar Chinese exports (*e.g.* tea).

## II

In the absence of estimates of Chinese national income over a series of years a direct relationship between the volume of imports and $f$ was computed:

$$m = 0{\cdot}81\,f \qquad R = 0{\cdot}88$$

The relatively high international reflection ratio

CHINA

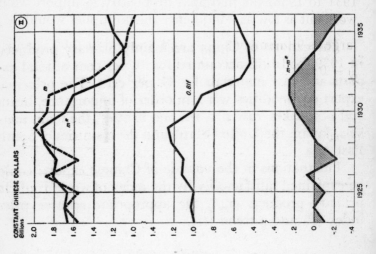

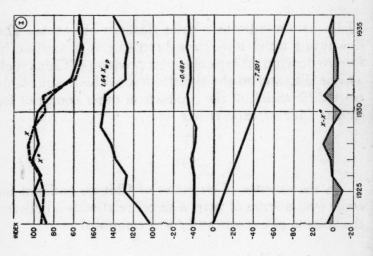

found (0·81) should be seen in conjunction with an estimate which may be made for the marginal propensity to
import. Using P. S. Ou's[1] figures on national income for
1931 to 1936, the marginal propensity to import would
work out as low as 0·09; hence the multiplier would be as
large as 9 $\left(\text{namely, } \dfrac{0·81}{0·09}\right)$ and $\delta$ would be 0·02 (namely.
$\dfrac{1}{9} - 0·09$).

[1] "The National Income of China, 1931 to 1936" (in Chinese). Figures repro-
duced in United Nations, *National Income Statistics of Various Countries*, 1938–1947
(Lake Success, 1948).

# INDIA

## I

India exports mainly primary products and some of her manufactured exports, such as the manufactures of jute, have only a rather small value added in the manufacturing process. It seemed reasonable therefore to use the index of the volume of world trade in primary products as the main explanatory variable for fluctuations in India's exports. Two other variables were used, an index number of the volume of export crops (computed as a weighted average of the cotton, tea and rice crops, the weights derived from the average relative importance of these three commodities in exports) and a trend break between 1930 and 1931 $(T)$. The result was as follows:

$$x = 0.48 \, x_{wp} + 0.22 \, h - 12.6 \, T \qquad R = 0.86$$

No statistical evidence of an effect of relative prices could be found but the trend break series may represent, among other things, a loss of markets in manufactured goods on account of Japanese competition in South East Asia.

## II

No reliable estimate for the national income of India over a series of years is available. A direct correlation between the volume of imports and $f$ was therefore made:

$$m = 0.65 \, f \qquad\qquad R = 0.88$$

The value 0.65 for the international reflection ratio appears rather low; but the correlation is relatively poor so that the coefficient found has a wide margin of error.

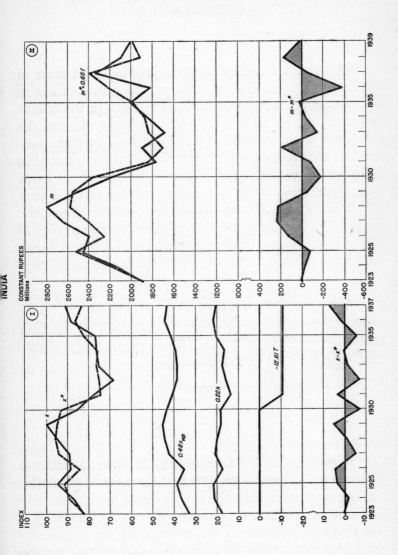

# INDONESIA

## I

The exports of Indonesia consist almost entirely of primary products. The six main exports, which accounted for 72 per cent of exports in 1937, are shown below:

|  | *Per cent of Total Exports* |
|---|---|
| Rubber | 32 |
| Petroleum | 15 |
| Tin | 8 |
| Copra | 7 |
| Sugar | 5 |
| Tea | 5 |
|  | 72 |

A good explanation of the fluctuations in exports could be obtained on the basis of fluctuations in the world trade in primary products and a trend which showed rather a high positive slope:

$$x = 0{\cdot}80 \; x_{wp} + 1{\cdot}70 \; t \qquad\qquad R = 0{\cdot}98$$

## II

In correlating real income with the foreign factors for a country like Indonesia which remits abroad the bulk of its export profits, both the export figure and the national income figure should be taken net of such profits. Normally these profits may be included in the definition of national income and they are, of course, always included in the value of exports. But while the remainder of the value of exports such as payments to producers, wage

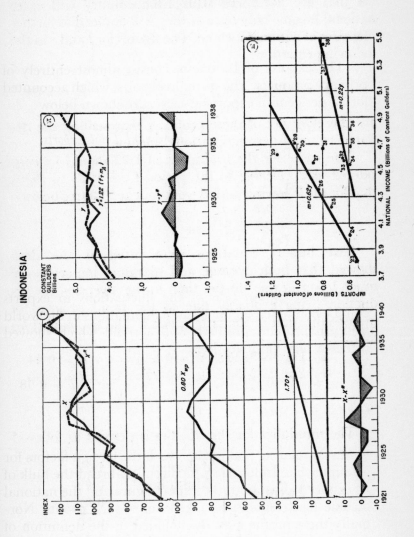

INDONESIA

payments, etc., may be expected to have a multiplier effect because they are spent in the country, export profits that are not spent within the country will enter national income only once as they will not lead to further increases of national income. The figures for $f$ and $y$ in the following equation:

$$y = 1 \cdot 22 \ (f + m_A) \qquad\qquad R = 0 \cdot 84$$

are therefore net of these profits, $y$ representing the deflated value of personal national income.

The value for the multiplier of $1 \cdot 22$ should be considered as applicable to the period from 1923 to 1930; that for the following period works out at $2 \cdot 28$ (see below).

### III

Two import equations were fitted as the data showed that both average and marginal imports were much lower in the 'thirties than in the 'twenties, the reduction being probably due to the rapid progress of industrialization in the latter period. The two equations follow:

(a) For 1923–30:  $m = 0 \cdot 62 \, y$ $\qquad$ $R = 0 \cdot 94$
(b) For 1932–38:  $m = 0 \cdot 22 \, y$ $\qquad$ $R = 0 \cdot 90$

### IV

The multiplier for the 'thirties is derived as follows:

|  |  |  |
|---|---|---|
| 'Twenties | Multiplier | 1·22 |
|  | (Multiplier)$^{-1}$ | 0·82 |
|  | $\mu$ | 0·62 |
|  | $\delta$ | 0·20 |
| 'Thirties | $\mu$ | 0·22 |
|  | (Multiplier)$^{-1}$ | 0·42 |
|  | Multiplier | 2·28 |

# JAPAN

## I

Raw materials and manufactured products were about equally important in the exports of Japan in the interwar period. In 1929 raw material exports accounted for 42 per cent of total exports and manufactured exports for 49 per cent. Raw silk and metals were the most important raw materials, textile tissues and piece goods the most important manufactures. Japan's main markets were in the United States and in Asia.

On account of the balanced composition of the exports of Japan the index of total world trade $(x_w)$ was selected as the primary explanatory variable. The second variable included in the correlation is $P$, the ratio of the price of Japanese exports over the price index of world trade in general. The result found was as follows:

$$x = 1 \cdot 04 \, x_w - 1 \cdot 26 \, P \qquad\qquad R = 0 \cdot 93$$

It will be noted from the diagram that price fluctuations explain a large part of the fluctuations in $x$; nevertheless the mean elasticity as it resulted from the calculation $(-1 \cdot 26)$ was only slightly in excess of unity. To the extent that reliance may be placed on this figure it would appear to indicate that although Japan was quite successful in increasing the volume of its exports by underbidding its competitors, it was not able by this process to increase much its export income.

## II

In the explanation of fluctuations in national income in Japan account should be taken, in addition to $f$ and

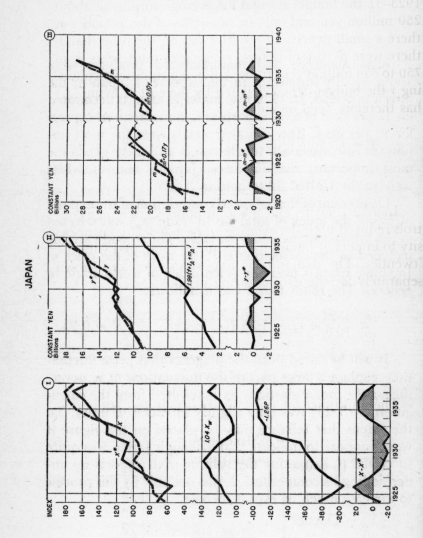

$m_A$, of the striking difference in the budgetary policy between the 'twenties and the 'thirties. In the period 1923–31 the budget showed an average surplus of about 250 million yen and only in two years of this period was there a small deficit. In the 'thirties, on the other hand, there were persistent deficits ranging in most years from 750 to 850 million yen. In the following equation explaining $y$ the budget deficit deflated by the cost of living ($I_A$) has therefore been included:[1]

$$y = 1 \cdot 98 \; (f + I_A + m_A) \qquad\qquad R = 0 \cdot 97$$

### III

Increased tariffs and the imposition of exchange controls reduced both the average and the marginal propensity to import of Japan in the 'thirties compared with the 'twenties. The demand for imports is therefore shown separately for the two following periods:

(a) 1921–29    $m = 0 \cdot 17 \, y$        $R = 0 \cdot 91$
(b) 1930–37    $m = 0 \cdot 10 \, y$        $R = 0 \cdot 97$

### IV

The multiplier for the 'thirties is found as follows:

| | | |
|---|---|---|
| 'Twenties | Multiplier | $1 \cdot 98$ |
| | (Multiplier)$^{-1}$ | $0 \cdot 51$ |
| | $\mu$ | $0 \cdot 17$ |
| | $\delta$ | $\overline{0 \cdot 34}$ |
| 'Thirties | $\mu$ | $0 \cdot 10$ |
| | (Multiplier)$^{-1}$ | $\overline{0 \cdot 44}$ |
| | Multiplier | $2 \cdot 22$ |

[1] The coefficient 1·98 in this equation represents the multiplier applicable to the 'twenties; the multiplier for the 'thirties is computed below at 2·22.

# ARGENTINA

## I

Argentina's exports are concentrated on a limited number of primary products, the most important of which, in 1937, were the following:

|  | Per cent of Total Exports |
|---|---|
| Corn | 26 |
| Wheat | 21 |
| Meats | 14 |
| Oil seeds | 12 |
| Wool | 7 |
| Hides and skins | 6 |
| Total | 86 |

No success was achieved by attempts to explain fluctuations in the volume of exports of Argentina by means of the index of world trade in primary products and the relative prices of Argentina compared with world prices of primary products. It appeared necessary to use in the correlation explaining fluctuations in Argentine exports three other series:

(a) a series $m_{f(UK)}$ representing the volume of British food imports. In 1937, 29 per cent of total exports of Argentina went to the United Kingdom.

(b) a series $h$, representing the crops of corn and wheat.

(c) a trend break ($T$) indicating a lower level of exports in the years from 1932 on compared with the preceding years, which may perhaps be attributed to the effects on Argentina of Imperial Preference.

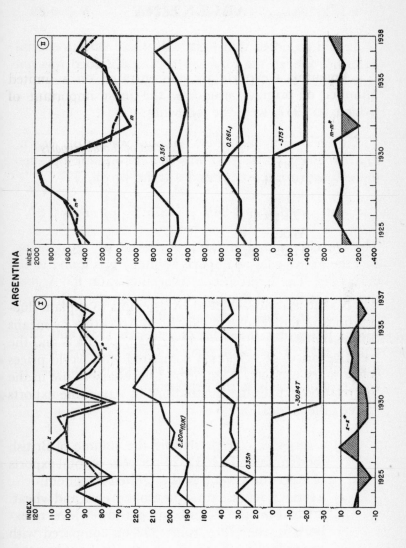

ARGENTINA

K

The explanation found on this basis was as follows:

$$x = 2 \cdot 20 \, m_{f(UK)} + 0 \cdot 35 \, h - 30 \cdot 84 \, T \qquad R = 0 \cdot 89$$

It will be noted that even with these various special series introduced the total correlation obtained was not very high.

## II

No series is available for national income in Argentina. A direct correlation was therefore made between the volume of imports, $f$, and a trend break, $T$:

$$m = 0 \cdot 35 \, f + 0 \cdot 26 \, f_{-1} - 375 \, T \qquad R = 0 \cdot 97$$

The correlation was notably improved by introducing $f_{-1}$; the average lag of imports behind $f$ was found to be $0 \cdot 43$ year. The international reflection ratio for Argentina on the basis of the first two terms on the right-hand side of the equation works out at $0 \cdot 55$.[1] The term with $T$ would indicate a trend break between 1931 and 1932 equivalent to 375 million pesos at constant prices, reflecting probably the exchange and trade controls introduced by Argentina early in the depression.

---

[1] *Cf.* page 70.

# CHILE

## I

Diagram Ia compares the volume of exports of Chile with the volume of world trade in primary products, both series as index numbers on the basis 1929 = 100. Two lines have been drawn in this diagram, one connecting the points from 1923 through 1929 and the other connecting the points from 1934 to 1938. These two lines appear to indicate two different relationships, both with fairly high correlation, but with a much steeper slope in the 'thirties than in the 'twenties. The interruption of the connecting lines in the early 'thirties will be discussed later. The preponderance of two items in Chilean exports, nitrate of soda and copper, which accounted for 55 and 27 per cent respectively of the value of exports in 1927, and for 19 and 56 per cent respectively of the value of exports in 1937, as well as the peculiar developments of nitrate exports, make it necessary to proceed to a somewhat more detailed analysis of Chilean exports.

Diagram Ib compares export of nitrates with the volume of world trade of primary products, both series again on the basis 1929 = 100. The diagram shows a rather steady relationship for the years 1923 to 1925 and 1928 to 1929, with a severe break in 1926 and 1927, years when the demand for nitrates from the United States was unusually low on account of depressed conditions of United States cotton growers. A new relationship, again rather close, is seen for the years 1930, 1931, and 1934 to 1938. During 1932 and 1933, however, the figures indicate a serious fall of exports and a subsequent recovery reflecting probably the disintegration of the nitrate cartel arrangements and the subsequent reorganization of the

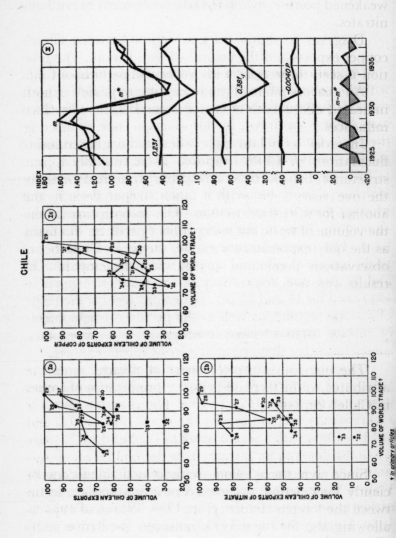

cartel. The level of nitrate exports in the 'thirties was much lower than in the 'twenties on account of Chile's weakened position owing to the development of synthetic nitrates.

Diagram Ic shows the connection between Chile's copper exports and the volume of world trade. The relation is seen to be close with a steep slope of about 4·5.

An analysis made of the remainder of Chile's exports indicated effects both of crop fluctuation and of cyclical influences.

In order to isolate the cyclical factors determining fluctuations in Chile's exports, as distinguished from structural changes, two correlations were made, one for the five years 1923 to 1925 and 1928 and 1929, and another for the period 1930 to 1937. In both correlations the volume of world trade in primary products was taken as the only explanatory variable, the limited number of observations precluding any further refinements. The results were as follows:

$(a)$ 1923–29:  $x = 1·03\, x_{wp}$      $R = 0·98$
$(b)$ 1930–37:  $x = 3·35\, x_{wp}$      $R = 0·80$

The increase in the regression coefficient should be attributed to the increased relative importance of copper in Chile's exports.

## II

Since no national income series is available for a sufficiently long period, a direct correlation was made between the foreign factors $(f)$ and the volume of imports, allowing also for the effect of changes in relative prices $(P)$:

$$m = 0·23\, f + 0·38\, f_{-1} - 0·0040\, P \qquad R = 0·97$$

The inclusion of the term $f_{-1}$, indicating a lagged response of imports to changes in the foreign factors, appeared useful. On the basis of the coefficients for $f$ and $f_{-1}$ the international reflection ratio was found at $0\cdot57$.[1]

In computing the price elasticity of imports from this equation account should be taken of the fact that the price coefficient in it is "net" of the multiplier effect.[2] Hence the elasticity coefficient corresponding to this equation (which is $-0\cdot31$) should be divided by $(1-\rho)$ to give an estimate of the price elasticity of imports of $-0\cdot72$.

[1] *Cf.* page 70.
[2] *See* Chapter III, equation (36·2).

# UNITED STATES

## I

United States export statistics are divided into five main groups. The distribution over these groups in 1937 was as follows:

|  | *Per cent of Total Exports* |
|---|---|
| Crude materials | 22·2 |
| Crude foodstuffs | 3·2 |
| Manufactured foodstuffs | 5·4 |
| Semi-manufactures | 20·3 |
| Finished manufactures | 49·0 |
|  | 100·0 |

It seemed useful to seek a separate explanation for the first three groups combined, most of which fall into the category of primary articles, and then for the fourth and fifth groups separately. In the first explanation some effect was found of relative prices $(P)$ and a trend $(t)$, in addition to the effect of fluctuations in the volume of world trade in primary articles $(x_{wp})$; in the second and third explanations the same variable $(x_{wm})$ was used and no significant results of other variables were found. The results of these three explanations were as follows:

Primary articles:
$$x_p = 0.31\, x_{wp} - 1.09\, P - 3.53\, t \qquad R = 0.96$$
Semi-manufactures:
$$x_{m1} = 1.15\, x_{wm} \qquad R = 0.88$$
Finished manufactures:
$$x_{m2} = 1.58\, x_{wm} \qquad R = 0.95$$

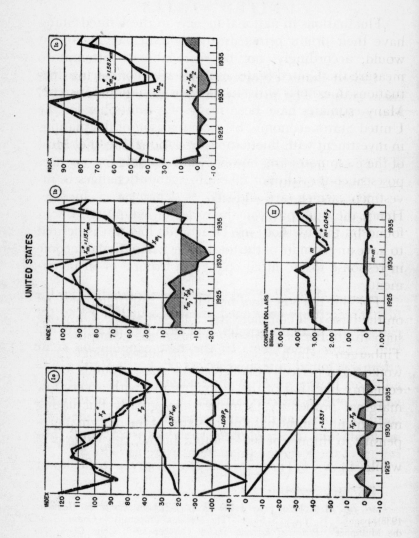

## II

Fluctuations in national income in the United States have their origin primarily in domestic factors and it would, accordingly, not be reasonable to attempt to measure the United States multiplier by comparing fluctuations in exports with fluctuations in national income. Many estimates have been made of a multiplier for the United States economy, by a comparison of fluctuations in investment with fluctuations in national income. Most of these estimates are, however, not suitable for our purposes since they do not take into account changes in investment which are induced by changes in income. Hence the multipliers in the order of magnitude 2 to 3 found by this method[1] are clearly too low if it is desired to have an estimate of the total change in national income in response to an initial change in exports or in investment.

For this purpose one should use a multiplier derived on the basis of a complete system of equations. Only one such multiplier is available, namely, that computed by Tinbergen,[2] which equals $5\cdot36$. This figure, though high, would seem perfectly plausible on *a priori* grounds for an economy like that of the United States with a very low marginal propensity to import and greatly fluctuating investment. On the basis of the value of the marginal propensity to import of $0\cdot045$ found below, the value of $\delta$ would be $0\cdot14$ $\left(i.e. \dfrac{1}{5\cdot36} - 0\cdot045\right)$, only a trifle lower

---

[1] *See*, *e.g.*, M. Kalecki, *Essays in the Theory of Economic Fluctuations* (London, 1938), page 73; R. N. and S. Stone, "The Marginal Propensity to Consume and the Multiplier", *Review of Economic Studies*, October 1940; Colin Clark, *The Conditions of Economic Progress* (London, 1938), page 476.

[2] J. Tinbergen, *Business Cycles in the United States*, *1919–1932* (League of Nations, Geneva, 1939), page 164.

than the values found for the United Kingdom and Germany.[1]

III

The following regression equation was obtained for fluctuations in imports:

$$m = 0 \cdot 045 \, y \qquad\qquad\qquad R = 0 \cdot 88$$

No statistical effect could be ascertained of either relative prices or of a trend. It will be noted that the correlation coefficient is not very high.

---

[1] It would be highly desirable to check Tinbergen's findings against those by Klein (Lawrence R. Klein, *Economic Fluctuations in the United States*, New York, 1950). No complete multiplier is available on the basis of Klein's model III which would be most appropriate for our purposes. An estimate can, however, be made on the basis of the equations in this model, making certain simplifying assumptions with respect to the movement of prices and some minor variables in his system, and postulating an approximate equation $T = 0 \cdot 30 \, Y$, in order to complete the system. $T$ represents a number of secondary variables of which business taxes is the most important. On this basis an estimate for the multiplier of $3 \cdot 4$ for the interwar period was obtained. It would not seem obvious that this estimate, though more recent and derived by more refined methods, is more reliable than the one readily available from Tinbergen's study; in any case the international system as a whole is not greatly sensitive to relatively small changes in the United States multiplier on account of the small value for the marginal propensity to import.

# EXPLANATION OF TABLE

*General.*—Unless otherwise indicated, all correlations refer to the interwar period, roughly 1924–38. The letters A and B indicate a decomposition of the interwar period into two parts, roughly the 'twenties and the 'thirties.

*Column* (1).—P = primary, M = manufactures, T = total. Indicates world trade series with which either total exports of country or groups of exports indicated have been correlated. For France, the United Kingdom, and the United States the figures on the T line have been found by addition of corresponding P and M coefficients. For the United States P stands for exports of crude and manufactured foodstuffs and crude materials, correlated with world trade in primary articles; $M_1$ for exports of semi-manufactures and $M_2$ for exports of finished manufactures; the latter two series were both correlated with the world trade in manufactures. (P) = country exporting primary articles but corresponding world series not used in correlation selected.

*Column* (2).—Elasticity of demand for country's exports.

*Column* (3).—Marginal propensity to purchase from country.

*Column* (4).—Price elasticity of demand for country's exports.

*Column* (5).—Other variables used in explanation of exports:

$$t = \text{trend}$$
$$T = \text{trend break}$$
$$h = \text{harvest}$$
$$m_{f(UK)} = \text{index of food imports in the United Kingdom}$$
$$\text{lag} = \text{corresponding world trade series in year } -1.$$

*Column* (6).—Correlation coefficient in export equation.

*Column* (7).—Multiplier.

*Column* (8).—Correlation coefficient in multiplier equation. (As multipliers for the Netherlands and the United States were not obtained by direct correlation, no entry is made for R for these countries.)

*Column* (9).—Marginal propensity to import.

*Column* (10).—Price elasticity for imports.

*Column* (11).—Other variables used in explanation of imports [see explanation of Column (5)].

*Column* (12).—Correlation coefficient in import equation.

*Column* (13).—International reflection ratio obtained as multiplier × marginal propensity to import for countries for which these coefficients are shown. For other countries obtained by direct correlation.

*Column* (14).—Correlation coefficient where $\rho$ was obtained by direct measurement.

*Column* (15).—Column (3) × Column (13).

*Column* (16).—$\delta = \dfrac{1}{\text{multiplier}} - \mu.$

# CHAPTER VIII

# SUMMARY OF RESULTS

## 1. SUMMARY TABLE

THE adjoining table presents in summary form the most relevant results of the findings for the twenty-five countries analysed in the preceding chapter. The table is divided into four sections. The first section summarizes the information with respect to the equations explaining fluctuations in exports; the second section, the information on the explanation of fluctuations in income (the multiplier); the third section summarizes the data on the import equations; and Section IV contains a number of derived coefficients. Only the most important parameters are shown explicitly in the table, namely, the "income"-type coefficients ($\xi$, $\sigma$, the multiplier and $\mu$), and the price elasticities; the latter more because it is desirable to have a summary presentation of all figures found than because they are of great consequence in our system. The coefficients found for $t$, $T$, $h$, and a number of other secondary variables are not shown explicitly although columns (5) and (11) indicate which of these variables are used in each equation.

It may be convenient to discuss the sections in the order in which they are shown.

## 2. EXPORTS EXPLANATIONS

It is clear from column (6), showing the correlation coefficient obtained in the explanations of exports, that these explanations are on the whole more satisfactory

157

when the explanatory factor is the world trade in manufactured products or total world trade, than when world
trade in primary articles is the explanatory factor. In the
former cases, that is for countries whose exports consist to
a considerable extent of manufactured products, the correlation coefficient is equal to, or larger than, 0·90 in nine
out of twelve cases. In the explanations of primary exports, on the other hand, although a large number of
calculations shows a high degree of correlation (eleven
out of eighteen cases have a value of $R$ equal to, or larger
than, 0·90), there are four countries for which the value
of $R$ was found to lie between 0·78 and 0·89, and in three
cases, Denmark, Australia, and Argentina, no satisfactory explanation could be obtained on the basis of
world trade in primary articles as the main explanatory
variable. These three countries export mainly primary
articles of animal or vegetable origin; for other countries
with similar primary exports the explanation is also poor.
The explanation of fluctuations in exports is, on the other
hand, more satisfactory for countries exporting primary
articles originating in mines or factories. Much more research will be necessary to obtain a satisfactory explanation of the exports of non-mineral primary articles; this
will almost certainly require an analysis of market
conditions for individual commodities.

The coefficient $\xi$ shown in column (2) may be considered as an "income elasticity"; it indicates the percentage change in exports of a country associated with a 1
per cent change in world trade (in primary articles,
manufactured articles, or world trade as a whole, as the
case may be). It was to be expected therefore that the
values found for $\xi$ would lie around a value of 1·00.
Actually their distribution around unity is very striking.
Of the twenty-seven coefficients found, fifteen lie between
0·75 and 1·25; six are below 0·75 and six above 1·25.
Only a few extreme figures were found. The extreme high

(3·35) was for Chile's exports in the 'thirties. This value was based on a limited number of observations and the correlation coefficient was low. The extreme values on the other side are found for exports of primary articles by the United Kingdom and the United States (0·33 and 0·31 respectively).

In order to pass from $\xi$ to $\sigma'$ [column (3)] a number of steps are involved (see Chapter IV). The most important of these are (a) a transformation of units, from index numbers with the same base to figures in constant dollars, and (b) a transformation from trade in manufactures of primary articles to total world trade. The first step is obvious and need not be discussed further. The second transformation requires the use of two equations explaining $x_{wm}$ and $x_{wp}$ in terms of $x_w$, all three series being expressed in constant dollars. A correlation for the interwar period (1924 to 1938) in which a trend was also included yielded the following results (omitting constant terms):

$$x_{wm} = 0·58 \, x_w - 0·061 \, t \qquad\qquad R = 0·97$$

$$x_{wp} = 0·45 \, x_w + 0·091 \, t \qquad\qquad R = 0·94$$

If the three series $x_{wm}$, $x_{wp}$, and $x_w$ had been constructed in such a manner that $x_w$ was precisely equal to the sum of the two other series, the coefficients for $x_w$ found in the two equations would have added up to 1 and those for the trend to 0. The coefficients actually found in the two correlations do not precisely fulfil these conditions, due to rounding in the construction of the series, separate deflation of $x_{wm}$, $x_{wp}$, and $x_w$ and similar minor differences. For our purposes the trend coefficient is of no particular interest as we want to know the marginal distribution of trade at any particular moment of time. After a slight adjustment in order to have the two coefficients add up to unity the following equations were used to make the second step in the transformation:

$$x_{wm} = 0.56 \, x_w$$

$$x_{wp} = 0.44 \, x_w$$

These figures indicate a marginal propensity to purchase manufactured exports higher than the marginal propensity to purchase primary exports; however the ratio of the average propensities was the reverse. At the average of period prices, the average value over the period 1934–38 of world trade in manufactures was approximately $8 billion (old gold dollars), and of world trade in primary articles approximately $13 billion (old gold dollars). It follows from these figures that the elasticity of demand with respect to income for world trade in manufactures was twice as large as that for world trade in primary articles (1·45 as against 0·72).

Although we found for some countries two different values for $\rho$ in column (13) the importance of this coefficient in the adjustment from $\xi$ to $\sigma'$ is so small as not to make it worthwhile to give two different values for $\sigma'$ which might at most differ by one point in the last digit. Accordingly, only one value for $\sigma'$ is given, with the exception of Chile where there are two different values for $\xi$. The difference in the totals shown for $A$ and $B$ (the 'twenties and the 'thirties) in column (3) is entirely due to the difference in the coefficient for Chile.

In less than half of the export equations could a price elasticity of substitution with the proper sign be found. All elasticities that were found were quite small, with the highest absolute value at 1·56 and eight out of twelve of the elasticities below unity in absolute amount. As mentioned earlier, not much importance is to be attached to the price coefficients.

## 3. MULTIPLIERS

With respect to the multipliers found, little comment is necessary in addition to what was said in the sections on the individual countries. The high correlation coefficients shown in Section II are rather striking as the relationship measured is an indirect one. Of the eighteen values shown for $R$, twelve are equal to 0·95 or higher. Of the twenty-two multipliers found, one, that for Norway, is well below unity and should probably be discarded; four lie between 1·00 and 1·50, seven between 1·50 and 2, and eleven above 2. The multiplier for the United States, which was not found by direct correlation with foreign factors, shows the highest value in the table (5·36). Admittedly this value is rather uncertain, but in judging the *a priori* plausibility of such a high value, account should be taken of the low value for the marginal propensity to import in the United States.

## 4. IMPORT EXPLANATIONS

Of all the relationships used in this study, that between national income and imports is the most widely known and accepted. It is somewhat remarkable therefore that the results found for this relationship are by no means generally very good even after allowance is made for the possibility of lags, of trend terms, and of the influence of relative prices. Thus a correlation coefficient of less than 0·90 had to be accepted for the import equation of the United States, Germany, Switzerland, and Hungary. The difficulty to find significant price coefficients was even more striking in the import equations than it had been on the export side. A price coefficient is shown for three countries only; and in each case the elasticity is small (less than 0·50 in absolute amount).[1]

[1] For the price elasticity shown for Chile, see the text on that country.

There are many instances which point to a reduction in the level of imports, or a reduction of the slope of imports with respect to income, or both, in the 'thirties as compared with the 'twenties. Out of eighteen countries for which an import equation could be fitted, a trend break $T$ was introduced in five. For six others it proved necessary to split the period into two parts, and in all these latter cases the value for the marginal propensity to import in the 'thirties was found to be much lower than it had been in the 'twenties, as shown by the following recapitulation:

|  | Marginal Propensity to Import | |
|---|---|---|
|  | *In 'twenties* | *In 'thirties* |
| Finland | 0·93* | 0·27 |
| Australia | 0·49 | 0·23 |
| New Zealand | 0·65 | 0·40 |
| Union of South Africa | 0·57 | 0·40 |
| Indonesia | 0·62 | 0·22 |
| Japan | 0·17 | 0·10 |

* Doubt as to the accuracy of this figure was expressed in the section on Finland.

## 5. INTERNATIONAL REFLECTION RATIOS

For most countries the international reflection ratio shown in column (13) was obtained as the product of the marginal propensity to import and the multiplier. For seven countries, however, for which no usable national income statistics were available, ρ was estimated by direct correlation between the foreign factors and imports. For those countries a correlation coefficient is shown in column (14) which, considering the quality of the data and the very indirect nature of the relationship, may be considered as quite high.

The values found for $\rho$ vary from a low of 0·22 for Japan to a high of 1·17 for Italy. They are distributed as follows:

| $\rho$ | Number of Countries |
|---|---|
| 0·20 to 0·49 | 5 |
| 0·50 to 0·74 | 10 |
| 0·75 to 0·90 | 4 |
| 0·91 and up | 6 |

These data would seem to indicate that the great majority of the countries analysed are "stable" in the sense that the value of $\rho$ is considerably below unity.

Closely related to the international reflection ratio is $\delta$. Column (16) gives the values for this parameter. The values for $\delta$ may be expected to be closer together than those for $\rho$ since they do not depend on different values for the marginal propensity to import. Apart from a few extremely high values (0·78 for Norway and 0·64 for France, which should probably be attributed to faulty national income data), the values for $\delta$ lie within a relatively narrow range. For seven countries, including the United States, the United Kingdom, Germany, Netherlands, and Sweden, $\delta$ is between 0·10 and 0·19. Slightly higher values are found for Canada and Switzerland, and a slightly lower value for Czechoslovakia. It would seem, therefore, that for industrial Europe and North America the values for $\delta$ may be taken to lie around 0·15 with not too wide a distribution.

Australia, New Zealand, and the Union of South Africa, on the other hand, all show values for $\delta$ of approximately zero. Possibly in these relatively newer countries the marginal propensity to save is lower, or the marginal propensity to invest higher, than in the more mature economies of Western Europe and North America.

Unfortunately the data for $\delta$ are very scanty for the less developed countries. There is a very rough estimate for China at $0\cdot02$ and a figure of $0\cdot20$ for Indonesia. For Argentina, Chile, and India no estimate for $\delta$ is available in the absence of national income data. For the first two countries $\rho$ is in the order of $0\cdot5$ which means that $\delta$ must be approximately as large as the marginal propensity to import.[1] But Argentina and Chile are among the most advanced countries in Latin America and it would be particularly interesting to have data on $\rho$ and $\delta$ for the other Latin American countries.

## 6. THE WORLD MULTIPLIER

Column (15) shows the product $\rho\sigma'$, which, according to equation (51·6), is necessary to compute the multiplier effect in world trade. The objective in multiplying the $\rho$'s by the $\sigma'$'s is to obtain a weighted average of the $\rho$'s. Since exports have not been explained for all countries the sum of the weights is less than 1, and in order to obtain the weighted average $\Sigma\rho\sigma'$ has to be  divided by $\Sigma\sigma'$. This ratio works out at $\dfrac{0\cdot424}{0\cdot813}$ for the 'twenties, and $\dfrac{0\cdot418}{0\cdot820}$ for the 'thirties. Both fractions are very near to $0\cdot5$ and we may accept, therefore, this value for the average of $\rho$. This value would indicate that an initial autonomous increase in imports would lead to a further increase in world trade of approximately equal magnitude, and similarly that an initial reduction in imports would, through the operation of the international economic system, lead to a further reduction in world trade of about equal size.

[1] Since $\rho = \dfrac{\mu}{\delta + \mu}$

# 7. APPLICATION TO THE 1929–32 DEPRESSION

Our estimate for the world trade multiplier may be used to estimate to what extent the decline in economic activity in the United States between 1929 and 1932, and the resulting reduction in the supply of dollars, was responsible for the reduction in world trade in the depression. According to figures given in *The United States in the World Economy*,[1] the supply of dollars decreased from 7·4 billion in 1929 to 2·4 billion in 1932, or by 68 per cent. A comparison of the supply of dollars in terms of current dollars tends, however, to overstate the significance of the decline in real terms. The fall in prices between 1929 and 1932 made a lower supply of dollars adequate to purchase the same quantity of foreign resources and hence to maintain the same level of activity abroad. In the following paragraphs we shall try, therefore, to arrive at an estimate of the reduction in the supply of dollars by the United States in real terms, treating separately commodity imports, purchases of foreign services and capital movements.

(a) From 1929 to 1932 the volume of United States imports declined by 39 per cent. In 1929 United States imports accounted for about 15 per cent of world trade. Hence the decline in imports from 1929 to 1932 had a primary effect on world trade of about 6 per cent of the volume of world trade in 1929. On the basis of a world trade multiplier of 2 the total effect of the decline in United States imports on world trade would be 12 per cent of world trade. Actually world trade fell by 25 per cent from 1929 to 1932 so that about one-half of the decline can be attributed, directly and indirectly, to the decline in United States imports.

[1] Hal B. Lary, *The United States in the World Economy*, U.S. Department of Commerce, Washington, 1943, page 6.

L*

Since the international reflection ratio for the United States is very low the effect on United States imports of a reduction in United States exports may be neglected and the total decline in United States imports may be considered as autonomous with respect to foreign factors affecting the United States economy.

(b) The supply of dollars by the United States on account of other current transactions declined from slightly under 2 billion in 1929 to 1 billion in 1932. If account is taken, however, of the reduction in world market prices by nearly 50 per cent between 1929 and 1932, it would not appear that the supply of dollars in real terms showed a significant decline on account of invisibles.

(c) The following statistics on the United States balance of payments in 1929 and 1932 may be helpful in arriving at an estimate of the decline in the supply of dollars on capital account. The figures for the balance of payments residual which are most likely to represent also certain capital items are also shown:[1]

|  | (Millions of Dollars) | |
|---|---|---|
|  | 1929 | 1932 |
| A. *Long-term capital movements:* | | |
| (i) Net flow through change in U.S. assets abroad | − 636 | + 251 |
| (ii) Net flow through change in foreign assets in U.S. | + 358 | − 26 |
| Balance on long-term capital movements | − 278 | + 225 |

[1] Lary, *op. cit.*, Table I.

|  | *(Millions of Dollars)* | |
|---|---|---|
|  | *1929* | *1932* |
| **B.** *Short-term capital movements:* | | |
| (i) Net flow through change in U.S. assets abroad | − 200 | + 227 |
| (ii) Net flow through change in foreign assets in U.S. | + 196 | − 673 |
| Balance on short-term capital movements | − 4 | − 446 |
| Balance on all capital transactions | − 282 | − 221 |
| Balance of payments residual | − 384 | + 73 |

It would seem that only the figures on the change of United States assets abroad (the first line in A and B) would be relevant for our purposes. The outflow of $636 million in long-term foreign investment in 1929 is likely to have created income abroad of a similar amount, while the acquisition by foreigners of $358 million of long-term assets in the United States (presumably out of their savings or out of other assets) is not likely to have constituted a deduction of a similar amount in real investment abroad. The outflow of $200 million in short-term capital in 1929 should probably also be included in figuring the income creating supply of dollars; but the accumulation of $196 million of short-term dollar balances should not be deducted. It is not quite sure whether the outflow of capital from the rest of the world to the United States on account of repatriation of United States capital, both long-term and short-term, in 1932, should be considered as a negative item which reduced investment abroad below the level it would otherwise have attained. If the figures for 1932 are to be taken into account on that basis they should be expressed at 1929 prices, *i.e.* nearly doubled in amount.

If no account is taken of the repatriation of capital in

1932 and the income-creating supply of dollars in that year is therefore put at zero, and not at a negative figure, the reduction of the supply of dollars on capital account between 1929 and 1932 would be found at $836 million at 1929 prices. If the return flow were included the difference in the supply of dollars between the two years, expressed at 1929 prices, would be roughly double this amount. Part of the residual should probably also be interpreted as an outflow of capital in 1929 and an inflow in 1932. A figure of $1 billion at 1929 prices would seem therefore a low estimate for the reduction in investment abroad which could be attributed to a reduced supply of capital from the United States in 1932 as compared with 1929. Since the outflow of capital is not itself recorded in the statistics of imports of commodities the only reduction in world trade due to the reduced supply of capital would be its secondary effects. Assuming the average reflection ratio at 0·5, these effects would amount to another $1 billion at 1929 prices, or 3 per cent of world trade. It would appear therefore that at least 12 per cent plus 3 per cent, or 15 per cent, of the total decline in world trade of 25 per cent between 1929 and 1932 can be attributed to the depression in the United States and the reduction of capital outflow from the United States.[1]

If as much as three-fifths, and perhaps more, of the decline in world trade from 1929 to 1932 is attributable to events in the United States,[2] import restrictions would

[1] It is not necessary in this connection to discuss to what extent the reduction in foreign lending was causally related to the depression in the United States. On this subject see, for instance, Arthur Bloomfield, "The Mechanism of Adjustment of the American Balance of Payments: 1919–1929", *Quarterly Journal of Economics*, LVII, May 1943, pages 333–377.

[2] On the basis of a world multiplier of 2, the entire decline in world trade from 1937 to 1938 can be explained by the recession in the United States. From 1937 to 1938 United States imports declined by 30 per cent. As United States imports were about 12 per cent of world trade in 1937 this decline in itself had a primary effect on the volume of world trade of about 3½ per cent; its total effect, with a world trade multiplier of 2, would be 7 per cent of world trade, which equals the actual decline of world trade between 1937 and 1938.

assume a relatively minor role in the explanation of this decline. We have found ample evidence of the effect of restrictions on imports compared to the level of income. This in itself would not, however, provide an indication of the effects of these restrictions on world trade, as the restrictions themselves increased national income (provided unused resources were available). Hence the exclusion by country $k$ of particular imports to a value of \$1 million would actually reduce the value of imports by that country by only $(1 - \rho_k)$ million. The negligible effect which import restrictions may in certain circumstances have on the value of imports is seen most clearly for countries like Australia and New Zealand, for which $\rho$ equals about unity. Despite the reduction of the slope and the level of the import-income curve, these countries' imports in the late 'thirties were far above the level they had ever reached in the 'twenties.

# ANNEX I

We have used in the text (p. 22) the proposition that real national income may, with a high degree of approximation, be represented by the sum of two terms, one representing the external influences and the other the real volume of output for domestic consumption, *i.e.*:

$$y \sim \frac{X}{p_m} + c - m \qquad (A-1)$$

We shall now prove that the difference between the expression for $y$ at the right-hand side of (A-1) and the definition of $y$ is small.

We define real national income $y$ as money national income $Y$ deflated by a cost of living index $p$:

$$y \equiv \frac{Y}{p} \qquad (A-2)$$

Introducing the symbol $\lambda$ for the difference between the right-hand sides of (A-1) and (A-2):

$$\lambda = \frac{Y}{p} - \left( \frac{X}{p_m} - c + m \right) \qquad (A-3)$$

it can be shown that $\lambda$ is small.

The index $p$ may be considered a weighted average of an import price index $p_m$ and a price index of purely domestic goods $p_d$, with weights $w$ and $(1 - w)$ respectively:

$$p = wp_m + (1 - w) p_d \qquad (A-4)$$

Here $p_m = \dfrac{M}{m}$ and $p_d = \dfrac{C - M}{c - m}$.

If we assume that all imports are used in the production of consumer goods for domestic consumption and that changes in im-

170

port prices are fully reflected in the prices of the finished commodities in the production of which the import commodities enter, then

$$w = \frac{\overline{M}}{\overline{C}} \qquad (A-5)$$

where $\overline{M}$ and $\overline{C}$ stand for the value of imports and consumption in the base period.

We may now proceed as follows:

$$\lambda = \frac{Y}{p} - \left(\frac{X}{p_m} + \frac{C - M}{p_d}\right) = \frac{X + C - M}{wp_m + (1 - w)p_d} - \frac{X}{p_m} - \frac{C - M}{p_d} =$$

$$= \frac{X[p_m - wp_m - (1 - w)p_d]}{p \cdot p_m} +$$

$$\frac{(C - M)[p_d - wp_m - (1 - w)p_d]}{p \cdot p_d} =$$

$$= \frac{X(1 - w)(p_m - p_d)}{p \cdot p_m} - \frac{(C - M)w(p_m - p_d)}{p \cdot p_d} =$$

$$\frac{p_m - p_d}{p}\left[\frac{X(1 - w)}{p_m} - \frac{(C - M)w}{p_d}\right] =$$

$$= \frac{p_m - p_d}{p \cdot p_m \cdot p_d} \cdot \left[p_d X(1 - w) - p_m(C - M)w\right] \qquad (A-6)$$

The term between $\Big[ \quad \Big]$ may be greatly simplified if we may assume that

$$\frac{X}{C - M} \sim \frac{w}{1 - w} \qquad (A-7)$$

This will be so if

$$X \sim M \qquad (A-8)$$

and

$$\frac{M}{C - M} \sim \frac{\overline{M}}{\overline{C} - \overline{M}} \qquad (A-9)$$

For those countries for which the approximations (A-8) and (A-9) are fulfilled, we may then simplify A-6 as follows, using (A-7):

$$\lambda \sim - \frac{(p_m - p_d)^2}{p \cdot p_m \cdot p_d} X(1 - w) \qquad (A-10)$$

With the three indexes $p$, $p_m$ and $p_d$ in the order of magnitude of 1, $\lambda$ is therefore a fraction of $X$ in the order of magnitude of the square of the difference of the two indexes $p_m$ and $p_d$.

For example, assuming $w = 0\cdot2$, $p_m = 1\cdot25$, $p_d = 1\cdot10$ so that $p = 1\cdot13$, then

$$\lambda \sim -\frac{(0\cdot15)^2 \times 0\cdot80}{1\cdot13 \times 1\cdot25 \times 1\cdot10}\ X = -0\cdot012\ X$$

If the price indexes are below unity $\lambda$ will tend to be somewhat larger, but still small for moderate differences between $p_m$ and $p_d$. Thus for $p_m = 0\cdot75$, $p_d = 0\cdot90$ and hence $p = 0\cdot87$ we find that $\lambda \sim -0\cdot031\ X$.

The approximation used in (A–1) is, however, not satisfactory in situations where $M$ shows a movement sharply different from $X$. This was particularly noticeable in certain debtor countries (*e.g.* Germany) where an inflow of capital in the 'twenties was suddenly reversed into an outflow of capital in the early 'thirties. Hence $M$, which had first been in excess of $X$, became abruptly less than $X$. The fall which subsequently occurred in $p_m$ thus affected a value of imports well below the level of $X$; and deflation of $X$ by $p_m$ would yield an over-estimate of the effect on $y$ of the fall in $p_m$.

For cases such as these an alternative formula was used. Let us write:

$$y = \frac{X + C - M}{\dfrac{M}{C} p_m + \dfrac{C - M}{C}\, p_d} \tag{A–11}$$

where the weights for the two price indices are not assumed to be constant.

We now want to establish the effect on $y$ of changes in the external factors $x$ and $p_m$. Suppose that in the next year $x$ changes to $(x + \triangle x)$ and $p_m$ to $p_m + \triangle p_m$. (We are not here interested in the changes of $C - M$ and $p_d$). Then real national income in that year ($y'$) will be:

$$y' = \frac{X + \triangle X + (C - M)}{\dfrac{M}{C}\,(p_m + \triangle p_m) + \dfrac{C - M}{C}\, p_d} \tag{A–12}$$

The increase in real income due to these changes in external factors may then be approximated as follows:

$$\triangle f' = y' - y = \frac{\triangle X}{p} - \Upsilon\frac{M}{C} \cdot \frac{\triangle p_m}{p^2} \tag{A–13}$$

Not too much accuracy is lost by disregarding the difference between
$\frac{Y}{C}$ and 1 and writing, therefore:

$$\triangle f' = \frac{\triangle X}{p} - M\frac{\triangle p_m}{p^2} \qquad \text{(A-14)}$$

Using statistical values for discreet years we measure:

$$'_t - f'_{t-1} = \frac{X_t - X_{t-1}}{p_t} - (p_{m_t} - p_{m_{t-1}})\frac{M_t + M_t - 1}{2p^2_t} \qquad \text{(A-15)}$$

and then cumulate from an arbitrary initial value to obtain the series $f'$.

Since in most cases $M$ showed sharp fluctuations from year to year it was felt necessary to use an average of $M_t$ and $M_{t-1}$, as indicated in (A-15); but the more moderate fluctuations in $p$ did not seem to require averaging for this variable.

# ANNEX II

Most of the series used have been derived from international secondary sources, in particular:

LEAGUE OF NATIONS.—*Review of World Trade*, 1938 (series on volume and prices in international trade). Unpublished series on $x_{wp}$ and $x_{wm}$ as well as on the corresponding prices and values for years prior to 1929 were kindly made available by Mr. F. Hilgerdt of the U.N. Secretariat.

*Statistical Yearbook*, various years (series on value of trade, cost of living indices).

*Balances of Payments*, various years (series on invisibles and capital movements in the balance of payments).

UNITED NATIONS.—*National Income Statistics of Various Countries*, 1938–1947 (series on national income). National income data for years before 1929 were obtained from national sources mentioned in this U.N. publication; where no other series were available, estimates by Colin Clark (*The Conditions of Economic Progress*) were used.

In addition to these, the following special sources were used for the series indicated:

CZECHOSLOVAKIA.—*Monthly Bulletin of National Bank*, 1939, No. 1 ($y$). For 1925–28, $y$ was extrapolated on the basis of industrial production.

FINLAND.—National Bank of Finland, *Monthly Bulletin* ($y$).

FRANCE.—*Bulletin de la Statistique Generale de la France*, 1945, pages 450–453 ($x_m$ and $x_p$).

GERMANY.—*Wirtschaft und Statistik*, Sonderheft No. 14, 1934 (long-term and short-term capital imports).

HUNGARY.—M. Matolcsy and S. Varga, *The National Income of Hungary* ($y$).

NETHERLANDS.—Central Bureau of Statistics (correspondence), ($x$, $p_x$, $p_m$).

J. Tinbergen, "De schommelingen van de invoer, 1923–1938" [Fluctuations in Imports, 1923–1938], *Statistische en*

*Econometrische Onderzoekingen*, 1948, No. 2, pages 1–9 $(m, p_m, T')$.

F. A. G. Keesing, *De conjuncturele ontwikkeling van Nederland, en de Evolutie van de Economische Overheidspolitiek*, 1918–1939 [The Cyclical History of the Netherlands and the Evolution of the Economic Policies of the Government, 1918–1939], (balance of payments data).

SWEDEN.—Stockholm Economic Studies, *National Income of Sweden*, 1861–1930 $(Y, 1924–28)$.

Aars statsverksproposition, *Inkomsterne* $(Y, 1929–36)$.

UNITED KINGDOM.—*Board of Trade Journal*, various years $(x_m, x_p,$ and corresponding price series).

J. R. N. Stone, "Analysis of Market Demand," *Journal of Royal Statistical Society*, 1946 (for index of $y$).

*White Papers on Government Finance* (level of $y$ in constant £'s).

J. Tinbergen, *Statistical Testing of Business Cycle Theories*, Vol. I. *A Method and its Application to Investment Activity* (League of Nations, Geneva, 1939), pages 95 ff. (Number of houses built and index of construction costs. The product of these two series was brought on an absolute level on the basis of census data on the output of the building industry and then deflated by the cost of living index to arrive at the B series).

AUSTRALIA.—Colin Clark and J. C. Crawford, *The National Income of Australia* $(Y)$.

CANADA.—Canada *Yearbook*, 1936 and 1942 $(X,$ on calendar year basis excluding gold, and $p_x$: wholesale price of exports on calendar year base, $x = \dfrac{X}{p_x}$; also $M$ and $p_m$.)

*Dominion-Provincial* Conference, "National Income, 1937–40" $(Y)$.

UNION OF SOUTH AFRICA.—*Official Yearbook of the Union of South Africa*, various years $(x, m, p_m)$.

S. H. Frankel, "An Analysis of the Growth of the National Income of the Union in the Period of Prosperity before the War", *South Africa Journal of Economics*, June 1944.

INDONESIA.—J. J. Polak, *The National Income of the Netherlands Indies*, 1921–1939" (unpublished monograph), $(x, m, f, y)$.

JAPAN.—*Financial and Economic Annual of Japan*, various years $(I_A)$. Mitsubishi Economic Research Bureau, *Monthly Circular*, 1937 and 1938 $(Y)$.

UNITED STATES.—*Statistical Abstract of the United States*, various years (foreign trade volume and price series).

For $Y$: Kuznets' series up to 1928, "old" Commerce Department series 1929 to 1938.

# INDEX

*ST indicates the Synoptic Table following page 157.

# INDEX

## AUTHORS